Praise for *Transformational Hispanic Marketing*

"We all are chasing growth. This book provides sound thinking on unlocking growth with Hispanic consumers."

— John Alvarado, Former SVP of Brand Marketing, Constellation Brands

"*Transformational Hispanic Marketing* challenges conventional wisdom and should be required reading for anyone marketing to Hispanics."

— Gregory Edwards, President & Chief Operating Officer, UniWorld Group

"*Transformational Hispanic Marketing* shines a spotlight on a significant opportunity. Any marketer looking for an effective roadmap for how to pursue this opportunity will find it in this book."

— Yvette Morrison, Global Head of Marketing & Brand, Caterpillar Inc.

"A must read for any marketer that is serious about growing share with this critically important segment."

— Anup Shah, VP/CMO Juice+ Brands at PepsiCo Beverages North America

TRANSFORMATIONAL HISPANIC MARKETING

Cultivating a More Strategic Approach

Sean Javier Martín

Copyright © 2021 Sean Javier Martín

No part of this publication may be reproduced, stored, or introduced into a retrieval system, or transmitted, in any form, or by any mean (electronic, mechanical, photocopying, recording, or otherwise), without the prior permission of the author.

ISBN: 979-8-736-96388-1

*To Judy, Kaley, Tyler, and Cole, who have transformed my life.
Thank you.*

CONTENTS

	Introduction	ix
1	An Overview of THM	1
2	Establishing the Hispanic Business Case	11
3	The Hispanic Functional Plan	25
4	Mapping the Starting and End Points	37
5	The Complicated Role of Culture	45
6	It Takes More Than Marketing	57
7	Hispanic Performance Tracking	65
8	Hispanic Research Pitfalls	77
9	With Whose Army?	89
10	Shared Accountability	105
11	The Hispanic Socialization Plan	109
	Afterword	*115*
	Appendix	*117*
	Acknowledgments	*123*
	About the Author	*125*

INTRODUCTION

I always promised myself that if I ever wrote a book, I would start with the following story. Please bear with me, because at first the connection to the book's subject matter will not be readily apparent. It was early November in 2001, and 9/11 was still fresh on everyone's mind. For many of us, this time of anxiety led us to be exceedingly risk averse since the foundations of our reality had been shaken. But I was anxious to get out of my job and to leave corporate America.

So, I found myself sitting in an empty conference room in a nondescript office building along an industrial highway in Atlanta, anxiously looking at my watch and waiting for the final decision maker in the interview process to enter the room. I was eager for something different than my role at The Coca-Cola Company, but in one of the many ironies of the day, I was waiting to meet with the infamous former chief marketing officer of Coca-Cola, Sergio Zyman. We had never met, although I had seen him speak at a number of Coke town hall meetings and had always been intrigued by what he had to say.

My anxiety was partially mitigated by the fact that my previous interviewers at this firm had explained that this final interview was nothing more than a mere formality, and that Sergio never asked questions at this stage, but rather focused on letting the interviewee ask questions of him. As a result, I did little prep, having naively assumed that my job offer was in the bag. Thirty minutes after the scheduled start time, in walked Sergio in a state of haste. He sat down bizarrely close to me, and immediately started firing off questions. I was caught flatfooted at first, but eventually readjusted and found myself really enjoying the dialogue.

About an hour into the interview, Sergio peeked at his watch and fired off one last question, and a relatively easy and predictable one at that: "Sean, who do you admire?" I took a minute to gather my thoughts since I literally had not been asked this question since my undergraduate interviewing days over a decade earlier. I quickly ran through the options in my head: Gandhi? Martin Luther King? A family member? These were all too predictable. Given that the discussion thus far has gone so well, I cockily believed I had built some equity with him and decided to roll the dice.

"Moses," I answered and awaited his reaction.

His face scrunched up as if he had sucked on a lemon, and he practically shouted back "Moses?"

In the subsequent minute of complete silence, I was convinced that I had blown it. I had committed the cardinal sin of inserting religion into a business interview.

He finally broke the silence and proclaimed in his unique accent, "Moses? Do you want to know something about Moses? Moses was an asshole!" He intentionally paused as if waiting for my reaction, and I tensed up thinking now that I was destined to return to Coke. But out of nowhere, he emphatically added, "But he was my hero!" What a roller coaster! I went from an all-time interview low to an all-time, yet very unexpected, interview high in the span of sixty seconds. He elaborated on his personal views of Moses for the next 10 minutes, at one point explaining how he thought of himself as a Moses-like figure, someone who could figuratively lead business people to the promised land of marketing-driven growth.

This anecdote might seem like just an entertaining tangent—but in reality, this interview set me on the path to developing my own theories about Hispanic marketing. While I had started my post-business school career in multicultural marketing for Gatorade, I had mostly avoided the multicultural arena for eight years, fearing that such roles might pigeonhole me. I did not want to be the "Hispanic marketing guy." Yet during my tenure at this consultancy, I reawakened to the promise of Hispanic marketing.

The thesis of this book is that Hispanic marketing is fundamentally broken, is not keeping up with general market efforts and thus needs to be reformed. Not only does Hispanic marketing rely too often on tired tropes, it is frequently riddled with compromises that hold the effort back. I've experienced this firsthand during my years of working in both general market and Hispanic market contexts. In this book, I advocate my philosophy of "Transformational Hispanic Marketing" (THM), which is about changing how we collectively think of and practice Hispanic marketing. THM involves embarking on a serious, prolonged, organization-wide shift in strategy, in order to more effectively engage the Hispanic market opportunity. This book shows how Hispanic marketing efforts have often been based on limited analysis and planning, simplistic implementation, and minimum measurement. This book focuses on what I believe is missing; those foundational and strategic capabilities that will help modernize and advance this field.

This is not a book that reinforces all of the old tropes common to Hispanic marketing efforts. It is instead focused on bringing some much-needed discipline and rigor to the field. In contrast to what many Hispanic ad agencies tend to focus on, this book does not focus on how to develop one breakthrough, "big idea" that will drive Hispanics to your brand. There will be no silver bullet solution that makes Hispanics engage more with your marketing efforts. This book does not concern itself with following conventional wisdom. This book appropriately calls B.S. on certain longstanding behaviors and encourages the Hispanic marketing industry to take a long look in the mirror.

I have written this book with two primary audiences in mind that make up the Hispanic marketing industry:
1. The Hispanic marketing practitioners at companies.
2. The service providers such as Hispanic ad agencies, research firms, and consultancies.

Ultimately, this book is for anyone that is looking to improve the effectiveness of their Hispanic marketing efforts. To those readers whose primary exposure to Hispanic marketing has come through the ad agency world, I recognize that some of what is detailed in this book might initially not seem applicable, but I'm out to show you that this approach is fundamentally sound and effective.

I also hope to establish upfront what this book is and is not. This book sets forth a philosophy on how to market to Hispanics, and more importantly, how to build an effective Hispanic marketing capability that is sustainable over the long term. On the other hand, this book is not intended to be a resource that cites all of the compelling demographic statistics, as there are plenty of helpful resources already available. This book is not a Hispanic cultural narrative, as that has already been well covered by experts such as Dr. Felipe Korzenny, the founder and director of the Center for Hispanic Marketing Communication at Florida State University and author of Hispanic Marketing: A Cultural Perspective. This book is also comprehensive in scope, as it is not focused on any one dimension of Hispanic marketing, but rather examines what it takes to win across a number of important capability dimensions, most of which actually precede the creation of marketing programming.

This book is not intended to resemble an academic journal, but is instead a practical guide written from the perspective of a marketing practitioner who then turned into a consultant and a researcher. My extensive experience as a service provider comes into play, but so does my experience as a marketing practitioner while at Gatorade, Coca-Cola, and Miller Brewing. I did not set out to write a long-winded tome. There is too much esoteric propaganda out there that makes Hispanic marketing seem indecipherable and impossibly complex—something you can't figure out on your own. Hopefully this book will take some air out of those misleading approaches. I know this topic isn't easy—hell, the failures of so many top companies to get Hispanic marketing right makes that clear—but I don't think this topic should be mystified and cloaked in a bunch of insider jargon either.

I think it is important to establish why I am well-positioned to write this book and share a unique perspective on Hispanic marketing. In many ways, you could say that I've always been a "straddler." For example:

- On a personal level, as a native Spaniard who immigrated to the U.S., I have straddled two identities and two cultures.
- Working extensively in the U.S. and in Latin America, I have also straddled two hemispheres on a professional basis.
- Throughout my career, I have straddled two marketing orientations: the broader context of the total market and the Hispanic market.
- I've also straddled the two different marketing worlds: being a marketing practitioner at large corporations and small startups, as well as being a provider of marketing services.
- While not all of my consulting or research projects

have been focused on the Hispanic consumer, I have been involved with an unparalleled number of strategic Hispanic projects and have worked alongside some of the most accomplished people in this industry over the past twenty years. These varied experiences have provided me with a unique ability to compare and contrast Hispanic market efforts to total market efforts. I liken it to being a better overall fútbol player if you have a depth of experience playing both defense and offense—you gain a better understanding of the overall game.

I was born in Madrid and moved to the U.S. at the age of 12. Although I was wholeheartedly a Madrileño, I had grown up bilingual with a Spaniard mom and an American expat dad. As you can imagine, my thick Spanish accent did not immediately endear me to my new middle school classmates in—of all places—Goldsboro, North Carolina. It was abundantly clear to me from the onset that I needed to do everything I could to fit in, and do so quickly. I needed to assimilate.

So, I very quickly concealed my Spanish identity, ditched speaking Spanish, and dropped any reference to my middle name of Javier. My last name of Martín, though from my mom, was common enough in America to make it easy to not call attention to my roots. This was long before the more enlightened years of Latinization here in the U.S., and this part of North Carolina was far from accepting of immigrants. I can still recall one of my new classmates asking me if Spain was next to Puerto Rico—I knew right then that I was in trouble.

Luckily for me, the North Carolina stint was less than two years. We then moved to Northern California, then Long Island, and then finally settled down in Florida. Many summers I would return to Spain to spend time with relatives, but with every passing summer, it was clear that in Spain I was considered an American, while back here in the U.S. I was considered to be a foreigner. Some Americans simply thought of me as a Mexican. While I'm sure the Goldsboro, North Carolina public school system's geography curriculum has likely improved since then, feeling rejected in my new home, while also feeling increasingly different from those in my country of origin, pushed me even further to cloak my Hispanic identity. It wasn't until my mid-twenties and my first job out of business school that I started seeing things differently.

I got very lucky and landed a plum role at Gatorade during its emergence as a cultural phenomenon, and I was prematurely entrusted with the brand's multicultural marketing effort. All of a sudden, my understanding of the Spanish language and Hispanic culture was an asset. These were still the very early days of Hispanic marketing, but I was pleasantly surprised to be able to add a lot of value. It was a phenomenal formative career experience since it married underserved consumer groups with a company that had ample resources and good intentions.

While I was occasionally given Hispanic projects in subsequent roles, I did not engage deeply with any Hispanic effort again until my last role at The Coca-Cola Company. I was the global director of marketing for the Walmart business and had been discussing best practices with Procter & Gamble (P&G) since they were considerably further ahead of Coca-Cola in terms of how they had developed their relationship with Walmart. This led to an opportunity for Coca-Cola and P&G to co-lead an effort to help Walmart de Mexico develop a portfolio strategy for the various retail banners they had recently acquired. This project involved a lot of time in Mexico, and as such required a deep understanding of the Mexican consumer. It was a great learning experience on many levels, but the most important one was that it provided me deeper exposure to the Mexican people and culture. It laid the foundation for helping me better understand the U.S. Hispanic consumer of Mexican descent.

After my ten combined years at Gatorade and Coca-Cola, I joined Zyman Group, which was a marketing consultancy created by the former chief marketing officer (CMO) of Coca-Cola. It was at this professional services firm that my understanding of the Hispanic market blossomed as I launched both the Latin American and the "Marketing 2 Hispanics" practices. This simultaneous, cross-border experience would play an important role in shaping my perspective on Hispanic marketing in the U.S. While the work was taxing—often requiring 90 or more hours a week and weekly intercontinental travel—I have very few regrets about my time at the firm. It solidified my credentials in the Hispanic space as we consulted with blue-chip clients such as ConAgra, Wendy's, and Coca-Cola, who saw untapped potential in the Hispanic market.

I subsequently started my own insights and brand development consultancy, Brandiosity. A year into this experience, a former colleague of mine from the Zyman Group joined me and the business really began to hit its stride. He was a Cuban American who had previously run the Hispanic insights function at PepsiCo. Because of his experience and his steadfast commitment to the Hispanic opportunity, most of our projects shifted in this direction. While I was initially reluctant to be pigeonholed by clients as simply the "Hispanic guys," I soon embraced the designation, and we began operating as one of the few insights and strategy shops with a focus on the Hispanic market.

It was while leading Brandiosity that I assumed an interim role heading up the Hispanic business at Miller Brewing. This too forms an important basis for this book as I was fully embedded in the organization and essentially handed the keys to a very well-funded Hispanic business for an intense, six-month assignment. Despite the fact that this was an interim stint, it proved to be an invaluable opportunity, which allowed me to not only run a large Hispanic team and function, but also have the imperative to entirely reinvent it.

Randel "Randy" Ransom, Miller Brewing's CMO, had hired me in anticipation of Miller's upcoming merger with Coors Brewing. More specifically, Randy was now in a head to head competition versus his counterpart at Coors for the CMO role for the new entity, MillerCoors. Miller Brewing had decided to combine forces with Coors Brewing in order to better compete against the industry giant Anheuser-Busch which enjoyed an almost 50 percent share of the domestic beer market. Prior to becoming the CMO of Miller Brewing, Randy had been the interim head of the Hispanic effort in a similar role to what he hired me to do. So, he realized that his Hispanic expertise was a key differentiator, and that the contest to become the CMO of MillerCoors was consequently going to closely examine the results of his efforts to reinvent the Miller Brewing's Hispanic business. Before my appointment, the incumbent in the lead Hispanic role had struggled to meet Randy's very high expectations and thus there was much to be done prior to consummation of the joint venture. That's where I came in—I had to right the ship with a sense of urgency in order to optimize Randy's chances. This baptism by fire experience helped me develop and refine many of the guiding beliefs that form the basis of this book.

After the immersive Miller Brewing experience, I then went on to provide Hispanic marketing consulting services for a slew of blue chip clients including AutoZone, Dr Pepper Snapple Group, Capital One, Heinz, Corona Extra, Victoria, Modelo Especial, Casa Noble Tequila, Snap-on Tools, Amway, and Anheuser-Busch. However, in keeping with my positioning as a "straddler," I also landed a fair number of engagements that were not Hispanic-specific, which enabled me to continue comparing and contrasting efforts targeting the total market and the Hispanic market. Across these experiences—from my early days as a marketing practitioner to my more recent years as sought after consultant, from my Hispanic and non-Hispanic engagements alike—I have honed my own philosophy about how to cultivate a more strategic approach to Hispanic marketing.

I actually started writing this book over a decade ago, before business and life got in the way, and then managed to finish it in 2021 during the COVID-19 pandemic. The simple reason why I wrote this book is to address why Hispanic marketing efforts today largely fail: the prevalent compromises that hinder the effort along with the tyranny of lower expectations. But there are also two events that neatly encapsulate my goals for this book and my commitment to this philosophy.

Let me start by first sharing an experience of mine from a new business pitch a little over a decade ago. It was one of many experiences that got me wondering, "Maybe I need to write a book to expose all of the nonsense out there that is holding back the collective Hispanic marketing effort." A business associate and I were pitching a large telecommunications company on why they needed to segment (the process of dividing the target market into smaller, more defined groups in order to identify the most attractive target group) the Hispanic market first before developing their marketing plan. Halfway through our presentation, the company's vice president of marketing interrupted us to advocate his own surprising point of view.

"This is all fine, but guys, the golden age of Hispanic marketing is over and has been for years!" he said.

I could hardly believe what I was hearing, in part because he was a South African expat whose pronounced Afrikaans accent made him hard to understand. And I was a bit stunned since his declaration had come out of nowhere, essentially killing any momentum we had built across our many previous meetings. The rest of the clients began to nod in unison, as if the pesky consultants had been finally put in their place. His proclamation did not materially affect their need to conduct a segmentation study of the Hispanic market, but nonetheless, the folks in the room assumed from the VP's disdain that any further discussion would be a waste of time.

My colleague and I composed ourselves and asked the vice president to clarify what he meant. This former IT executive, who now held the reigns of the marketing function, felt that the heyday of Spanish language advertising was now past us since the Hispanic population in the U.S. was increasingly English-dominant. What he and his team failed to understand is that Hispanic advertising does not equal Hispanic marketing. They also failed to understand that there has been no "golden age" as of yet, although I hope this book might help move along the discipline of Hispanic marketing toward a more enlightened era—an era where Hispanic marketing is not immediately equated with Spanish language advertising and where Hispanic marketing is grounded in data about consumer attitudes and behaviors versus mere assumptions about cultural differences, as well as an age where Hispanic marketing becomes an enterprise-wide mandate versus something only the Hispanic marketing team is tasked with. It is time to bring more science to the field and leave the snake oil peddling behind.

While that experience first inspired me to think about taking on a book project like this, a more recent event cemented my conviction that I had to do something about the avoidable and repetitive mistakes I was seeing in the industry. On January 6th, 2020, I received an email with the heading "touching base" from a person whose name I didn't recognize. My first impulse was to move it into my junk email folder, but for some reason I thought to read down just in case it wasn't junk. As it turned out, it was from someone at a client company I hadn't worked with in seven years. This person (for the sake of confidentiality I will refer to him as Luis) wanted to set up time to chat with me about my firm's previous work for his company. I was floored. I do periodically hear from former clients, but I'd never heard from anyone seven years after the fact. I was intrigued by the opportunity to talk with Luis, since my firm had done some exceptional work for this company but had never been called back once our primary contact at the time took a job elsewhere shortly after we presented our last deliverable. As it turned out, Luis had just assumed a leadership role heading up Hispanic insights and strategy, which was a newly created position. While his new job description was not yet fully fleshed out, he had inherited a trove of legacy Hispanic documents, which he had perused as part of his initial due diligence. He had come across my firm's previous deliverables and was impressed by the extensive work we had conducted for his distant predecessor. I was very surprised he managed to read our seven year old documents, especially given that anything older than two to three years is typically considered to be stale in the fast evolving field of consumer marketing. Herein lies one of the typical stumbling blocks for Hispanic marketing: most institutional or acquired knowledge is not clearly identified, archived, protected, and carefully transferred as folks rotate through leadership roles.

After a number of phone conversations and an in-person meeting in lower Manhattan in late February, literally on the eve of the coronavirus pandemic, Luis hired me to help him activate his new role, and add strategic structure to his company's Hispanic efforts. One of my first tasks was to diligently audit the vast and disorganized information he had inherited, identify what we had to work with, and identify key gaps that would then inform his Hispanic learning agenda. I could not believe my good fortune. Not only had a significantly lapsed and very attractive client called completely out of the blue, and then hired me, but now I was given a unique opportunity to assess what they had done over the preceding seven years when it came to the Hispanic market. This provided a unique lens into the past, showing me not just how a large company managed the entirety of its Hispanic efforts, but also how it had evolved its approach to the Hispanic market across a significant period of time. So, I spent weeks going through dozens of lengthy PowerPoint documents created by a slew of well-known Hispanic agencies and prestigious management consultancies. As part of this literature review, I came to the following conclusions that solidified for me that I had to go back and finish this book once and for all:

- Their Hispanic fact base had a lot of unusable material in it. I liken it to all those cache files that accumulate over time on my computer that slow down its performance. My client's Hispanic fact base was cluttered with the oft-repeated Hispanic stats-facts-demographics, Hispanic marketing best practices, clichéd reviews of Hispanic passion points, and that sort of thing. But it was light on actionable insights and strategies that were relevant to their specific business and category.

- Once again, I saw a very familiar cycle repeated when it comes to Hispanic marketing. My client Luis, who was originally from Mexico but who had been in the U.S. for over 20 years, had been reassigned from his previous role as a brand director to this new insights and strategy role focused on Hispanics. Sound familiar? Yes, his primary qualifications for this very specialized role included being Hispanic and being fluent in Spanish. While he did have a considerable amount of experience with Hispanic marketing in previous roles, none of those had been hardcore insights and strategy roles, and most of his experiences were related to brand activation and the development of marketing programs and advertising. Luis admittedly lacked the functional expertise that was required in his new role. At many companies it's just assumed that if you are Hispanic, you innately know

how to market to Hispanics, which simply isn't true.
- The most significant learning that came out of this extensive literature review was that this company's Hispanic efforts had, subjectively, regressed since 2013. For a long time, this company had been at the forefront of Hispanic marketing and the envy of the industry. They had taken a significant step backward. Their historic strength with Hispanic consumers had weakened considerably and looking through these files painted a picture as to why. Thus, this book is not just about helping companies evolve their Hispanic marketing, it is also about helping companies minimize or avoid regression.

One of the other major factors that holds our industry back is the lack of precision and consistency when it comes to key designations. This is fairly common across all of marketing as we don't have the commonly accepted standards and language that accounting (e.g., GAAP, which stands for Generally Accepted Accounting Principles) and manufacturing (e.g., TQM, which stands for Total Quality Management principles) have. So, while this lack of precision is not unique to Hispanic marketing, I think that in combination with other factors that I will discuss in this book, it exacts a greater toll on Hispanic marketing's credibility than the credibility of marketing in general. I want to take a minute to get more precise in terms of several, foundational terms that are currently used inconsistently across our industry.

Hispanic vs. Latino Designations

When I claim that our industry has suffered from a lack of precision, I need to point no further than the fact that the terms Hispanic and Latino are frequently used as synonyms, sometimes even by folks who themselves are Latino or Hispanic, or both. But as Horacio Sierra, an associate professor at Bowie State University, made clear in a recent Washington Post op-ed: "The frequent use of the slashed term 'Hispanic/Latino' implies that the identities are interchangeable,"[1] when in fact, they are not. It's an easy pitfall to make—I know I've made the mistake repeatedly over the years—but when we collectively continue to conflate these terms, it highlights Hispanic marketing's lack of precision on something that is quite fundamental.

For clarity, "Hispanic" is a descriptor that stems from the word "Hispania," the Roman Empire's name for Spain, so it refers to the peoples and cultures of Spain and its former colonies. "Latino" describes the peoples and cultures where colonizers spoke Latin-derived languages, such as Spanish, French, and Portuguese. The term "Latin America" was coined in the 1800s to differentiate Romance-language-speaking areas from English- and Dutch-controlled territories, so people from Brazil (Portuguese) and Haiti (French) can be considered Latino but not Hispanic. Meanwhile, I am Hispanic given that I was born in Spain to a Spanish mother, and yet I also identify as Latino given that my great grandfather was Cuban. Only for the purpose of consistency do I use the term Hispanic throughout this book.

General Market vs. Non-Hispanic Designations

I want to call out another example of intellectual laziness that hovers around Hispanic marketing. I realize that in the grand scheme of all marketing, the Hispanic space is relatively new, which explains some of the underdevelopment in terms of consistency and rigor.

---

[1] Horacio Sierra, "Five Myths about Hispanics," *The Washington Post*, October 3, 2019, https://www.washingtonpost.com/outlook/five-myths/five-myths-about-hispanics/2019/10/03/1640cca0-e55c-11e9-a6e8-8759c5c7f608_story.html.

However, another of my pet peeves is the ever-shifting and loosely used term of "general market," which is often used as the comparison point for the Hispanic market (i.e., "when compared to the general market, Hispanics are more like to…"). To many, the term has come to represent non-Hispanics, while to others, it represents the broader or entire population, which is inclusive of Hispanics. And for others, the term is used in reference to what is essentially the English-speaking market or the non-Spanish speakers. What a mess! As practitioners of Hispanic marketing, we need to apply a clear and consistent set of definitions so that things are not left up to interpretation. I operate under the following interpretive distinctions:

- General market (sometimes referred to as the "total market"): The entire consumer landscape inclusive of all races and ethnicities; the total population base, which can be used as a basis for comparison. It is inclusive of Hispanics.
- Non-Hispanic market: Essentially represents the general market minus the Hispanic market, regardless of acculturation groups. I think this is the better frame of reference when contrasting Hispanic data. I will attempt to minimize the use of "general market" and use the phrases "non-Hispanic market" or "total market" throughout this book where possible to avoid confusion.
- Hispanic market: I know you are asking yourself if this really needs to be explained, but the answer is a definite "yes." I have seen too many companies use this term in reference only to Spanish-dominant Hispanics. For some reason, these companies choose to forget the bicultural and acculturated Hispanics.

Another area that tends to lack precise terminology is acculturation groups. The topic of acculturation could fill an entire book unto itself, but I have chosen not to debate it here given that this topic has essentially become a cottage industry. I'll give you a quick example of what I mean: as part of reviewing my client's Hispanic fact base back in early 2020, I found agency documents selling the concept of "Fusionistas" and "Ambiculturals." Different agencies used different terms, but each broadly refers to bicultural Hispanic young adults. Hispanic acculturation and the various models used in adjacency to distinguish unacculturated, bicultural and acculturated Hispanics can be fairly complicated and fluid. So, do we really need to make this even more esoteric by introducing new terminology like "Ambiculturals" and "Fusionistas?"

Now that I've established why I finally wrote this book, let's move onto Chapter 1, which provides a high-level overview of Transformational Hispanic Marketing.

1

AN OVERVIEW OF TRANSFORMATIONAL HISPANIC MARKETING

In reality, the Hispanic opportunity is essentially unattainable for most companies until they fundamentally change the way they think and behave towards this consumer group. Meaningful engagement with Hispanics should go from being a "nice to have" to being an "imperative;" from being a "nice to do" to being "must do." Hispanic marketing at many companies suffers from a vicious cycle, where a lack of strategic rigor creates variable or unmeasurable results, which in turn forces companies to constantly reconfigure their approach. This behavior invariably leads to regression…defined as a return to a former or less developed state.

Figure 1: Hispanic Marketing Vicious Cycle

For a cautionary tale of the failures of this approach, you need look no further than one of my former employers, The Coca-Cola Company, whose flagship brand has historically been considered by many to be best in class in its commitment to the Hispanic market. Over the years, the company has reorganized its approach to the Hispanic market several times while still benefiting from the pent-up demand for brand Coca-Cola that most Hispanic immigrants bring with them from their countries of origin, where Coca-Cola enjoys an even more vibrant business than here in the U.S. My perspective is grounded in the seven years I worked at Coke, and the subsequent consulting work my firm did for Coke. However, the following example could apply to any number of large companies:

Keep in mind that according to *The Wall Street Journal* and the executive search and leadership consulting firm Spencer Stuart the average tenure of chief marketing officers and others in equivalent roles at 100 of the top U.S. advertising spenders declined to about 41 months in 2020. CMO turnover is pretty common and frequent.

- Stage 1: A newly appointed CMO arrives and immediately conducts the due diligence regarding the overall marketing team and function they've inherited. As part of this assessment, when the CMO asks to see the results of the previous Hispanic marketing efforts, they are met with little information, which makes it impossible to conclude whether the Hispanic marketing was successful or not. So, the CMO understandably comes to the conclusion that previous Hispanic marketing efforts didn't work, and that something has to change. Not surprisingly the CMO then reconfigures the Hispanic marketing team and appoints a new leader.
- Stage 2: The newly appointed leader of the Hispanic marketing effort, who is understandably feeling a lot of pressure given their new role, immediately sets out to reinvent the company's approach to Hispanic marketing. This person feels that they have to quickly show the CMO that they are indeed doing things differently. Herein lies one of the ongoing problems—a quicksand of sorts—in that Hispanic marketing teams are constantly being reorganized as the function is prioritized, deprioritized, reinvented, subordinated, and typically underfunded.
- Stage 3: The new leader of the Hispanic marketing effort also feels compelled to hire a new Hispanic ad agency. After all, they feel a mandate to change things up, but have no specifics on what actually wasn't working in terms of the previous effort given the aforementioned lack of information. Hiring a new agency is a very visible indicator that they are taking

action and, of course, optics always matter.
- Stage 4: Significant resources are spent with the new ad agency on the development of a new ad campaign. As is too often the case, the new Hispanic ad agency is tasked with developing a new breakthrough campaign or a "big idea" in the absence of a tight creative brief from their client. Everyone feels great about the new work, which is very creative and culturally rich but is not grounded in a fundamentally sound, consumer-centric strategy (a key step that is often overlooked in this haste).
- Stage 5: The measurement systems in place continue to be inadequate and cannot effectively measure what impact, if any, this new Hispanic advertising campaign has had in the marketplace. It is simply impossible to assess the campaign's ROI.
- Stage 6: About a year later, as part of the annual resource allocation process, the CMO asks to see proof that the investment in Hispanic marketing made sense before funding it again at aggressive "investment levels" in the annual budget. Once again, the Hispanic team has no hard data but makes their best attempt at rationalization by falling back on the typical tropes about the rapid growth of the U.S. Hispanic population to support the investment or if they are lucky, the new ad campaign picked up some industry creative awards along the way. While somewhat compelling, this information is simply too generic and inadequate.
- Stage 7: As a result, the Hispanic effort gets less funding, and the team and effort are pared back…until the next CMO arrives and repeats the cycle. It's not hard to predict. The unproven investment eventually leads to more scrutiny and less funding. Hispanic marketing gets treated like a wager that didn't pay off.

In summary, the Hispanic marketing function is often

in flux, and the rest of the organization fatigues on this effort—the promises, the constant changes in direction, the lack of measurable results, the constantly shifting leaders and staffers. This in turn builds up organizational scar tissue. As a result, people in the broader organization get conditioned to not take future attempts to revamp the Hispanic marketing effort that seriously, and Hispanic marketers learn to expect frequent mandates to shift direction and varying degrees of engagement from senior executives. The same mistakes are repeated with each new leadership team.

In my experience, most companies accept a number of significant compromises that complicate the formation of an enduring and effective Hispanic marketing capability. Transformational Hispanic Marketing is designed to address these significant, self-inflicted compromises that often impede success and leave Hispanic marketing efforts unstable and ever-changing. THM is underpinned by a set of imperatives that are meant to address the following common compromises:

Compromise #1	Far too many people equate Hispanic marketing with cultural marketing. As a result, many Hispanic marketing efforts simplistically leverage cultural stereotypes and symbols versus doing the heavy lifting that is required to truly understand consumer wants and needs.
THM Imperative #1	THM believes that Hispanic marketing strategy should take culture into consideration but should not be driven exclusively or primarily by culture.
Compromise #2	Too many companies treat their Hispanic efforts as nothing more than the cost of doing business. They don't treat Hispanic marketing as

	imperative that will drive growth. As a result, the business case is often superficial, nonexistent, or too dated to be relevant.
THM Imperative #2	THM requires that an analytically rigorous and compelling business case be made. THM also requires that the Hispanic business case be updated periodically since ongoing support for the Hispanic effort is typically tenuous.
Compromise #3	Many companies don't clearly articulate what success looks like for their Hispanic business. This makes it hard to assess whether the effort is succeeding or not, and whether it deserves continued funding.
THM Imperative #3	THM requires that a company clearly articulate the winning ambition or destination for their Hispanic business. This in turn requires an accompanying understanding of what the current state or starting point is. Once you have a clear sense of your current reality and your destination, you can build a plan to bridge the two.
Compromise #4	The Hispanic function at many companies lacks a clearly defined role, and it is not crystal clear what the Hispanic business team owns and is accountable for.
THM Imperative #4	THM requires that the Hispanic effort be supported by a Hispanic Functional Plan that delineates the role of the Hispanic marketing team and how the function drives incremental value.

Compromise #5	Most companies can't accurately measure their Hispanic business and the resulting impact of their initiatives.
THM Imperative #5	THM requires that Hispanic business performance be isolated and tracked on a systematic basis in order to drive transparency and accountability.
Compromise #6	The Hispanic business imperative is typically owned exclusively by the Hispanic marketing team. Without broader accountability, the Hispanic effort will be siloed and will never reach its full potential.
THM Imperative #6	THM requires shared accountability across the enterprise—both vertically and horizontally.
Compromise #7	Institutional understanding of the Hispanic opportunity tends to be very shallow. Furthermore, institutional memory tends to be very short when it comes to the Hispanic effort. These inefficiencies dampen the ability for the effort to gain longer term momentum and scale.
THM Imperative #7	THM requires a disciplined socialization effort that helps broaden institutional knowledge and helps the organization not only retain its Hispanic knowledge, but build on it.

This type of transformative work can be contentious. It is not uncommon for sales and marketing to butt heads in this effort. In most companies, the Hispanic initiative is thought to be the sole responsibility of marketing, with both sales folks and marketers guilty of this misperception. The minute the Hispanic effort begins to be seen as a broader, commercial responsibility, the sales function tends to get its feathers ruffled by the prospects of added scrutiny.

Thus, embarking on a transformational process requires—at a minimum—a core team of cross-functional personnel. If possible, the implementation of Transformational Hispanic Marketing should also be facilitated by an objective, third party, which can avoid the traditional silos and turf battles so common within companies. An external facilitator tends to bring an external fact base and best practices, which can accelerate the process and lead to better outcomes. Keep in mind that there are a lot of firms and individuals out there that will position themselves as the right resource, but very few actually have the requisite experience to help a company truly transform its Hispanic efforts. I also caution companies against using their ad agency for this type of effort as this type of work is not their core competency. It is important to think of Hispanic ad agencies as creative experts, not capability builders or organizational design experts.

There's no better setting to observe the Hispanic marketing industry's dysfunction than any typical Hispanic or multicultural business conference. Now, why is it that so many Hispanic marketing teams feel obligated to attend each and every one of these conferences that they're invited to? Prioritizing such flashy, unnecessary events is sometimes tremendously counterproductive to the credibility of the Hispanic marketing effort. Sure, it is a lot of fun to spend a few nights at the Mandarin Oriental hotel in Miami and party on South Beach, but you aren't fooling anyone.

These events typically provide nothing more than opportunities for personal networking. They simply don't do much to drive the Hispanic business, and they are drain on time and money. As an occasional speaker and former advisory board member to the American Marketing

Association, I am familiar with how the industry works and why such conferences can be professionally appealing. And while they typically create a forum for vendors to present to potential clients, they rarely benefit the companies that sponsor them and send hordes of attendees. There is little value beyond the optics of sponsorship. I once worked with a new client that had been very upfront about the limited funds that were available for my firm's services, yet that same company sent five people (ironically, none of whom were principally involved in the Hispanic marketing function) down to Miami for one of these annual conventions. You do the math. Plus, beyond all the time and money that is diverted from more immediately meaningful tasks, what do all these company-paid vacations do to the broader perception of the Hispanic marketing team? If a company only sees Hispanic marketing as valuable insofar as it can be touted at an industry event, it's no surprise that so many Hispanic marketing programs lack strategic rigor and aren't taken seriously by other employees.

Let's take a minute to examine some of the presentation topics for one of the large multicultural conferences held during a recent summer in New York City:

- CMO perspectives: Building a purposeful, diversity-forward brand
- The culture-driven storytelling
- Culture-driven brands

Let's also examine some of the presentation topics for one of the large Hispanic conferences held a number of years ago, which was (I'm sure, just coincidentally) held in the winter, in (you guessed it!) Miami:

- Diversity and inclusion: key components to Procter & Gamble's growth strategy
- Leveraging diversity as a competitive business advantage

- Beyond demographics: Latino identity, and how it impacts media behavior
- Unlocking the secrets to great multicultural advertising

Now, what are the common themes across these two and many other conferences? Beyond the fact that so many presentations, so many years in a row, reiterate identical talking points about the importance of diversity and the power of culture, the presentations add little to our understanding of what Hispanic marketing is, and how it differs from other types of marketing. In essence, these presentations treat Hispanic marketing as synonymous with "cultural marketing," advertising and media efforts, and "diversity marketing." But in reality, Hispanic marketing requires efforts that are distinct from "diversity marketing," and all multicultural marketing efforts necessitate different strategies than advertising. This is marketing malpractice. Again, these examples of how conventional Hispanic marketing efforts go astray help explain why I wrote this book: to dispel the myths, debunk the jargon, and to slow—if not stop—the astounding, counterproductive levels of self-interest in this industry. I am simply stating that this field of ours needs more precision, rigor, and discipline. We need to stop shooting ourselves in the foot.

The following chapters will detail core elements of THM. It is important to keep in mind that THM is intended to be a modular in nature, so companies can prioritize whichever component parts work best for their specific operating context. But at the same time, it typically works best when the component parts are treated as a cohesive whole.

2

ESTABLISHING THE HISPANIC BUSINESS CASE

Why create a dedicated Hispanic marketing effort in the first place? Why is this consumer important? The Hispanic Business Case (HBC), which is a justification for the overall Hispanic undertaking on the basis of its expected commercial benefit, makes clear why a separate and dedicated effort is necessary. Obviously, the salience of the Hispanic opportunity depends on each company's or each brand's specific context. But with Hispanics representing 18.7 percent of the U.S. population as of 2020,[2] and with current demographic projections suggesting that the Hispanic population is growing and disproportionately young, most companies should instead be wondering, "Why aren't we *already* investing in dedicated Hispanic efforts?"

While the case might seem obvious in the context of this book, the burden of proof will—for the foreseeable

---

[2] United States Census Bureau
https://www.census.gov/library/stories/2021/08/2020-united-states-population-more-racially-ethnically-diverse-than-2010.html

future—be on the person or team advocating for this dedicated effort. After all, the key is to approach investing in the Hispanic opportunity like any other significant business investment. If someone at Georgia-Pacific recommends that a new paper towel production line be purchased and installed to address a sustained spike in demand, the immediate reply is going to be, "Can't our existing plant capacity handle the increased demand?" and "Where is the business case for that incremental investment?" Too many companies—and for that matter, too many Hispanic marketers—have treated investments in dedicated Hispanic efforts as a God-given right, something to be automatically renewed in the annual planning process. That type of mentality is nothing short of entitlement, and it will eventually not pass financial scrutiny. I know firsthand that Hispanic marketers all crave some degree of stability and would like to avoid the constant fits and starts that so often plague Hispanic marketing efforts. Well, the best way to inoculate ourselves from this lack of stability—from year to year, and from leadership team to leadership team—is to have a rock solid business case that documents why a robust, well-funded Hispanic marketing effort makes smart business sense.

The HBC will look different across companies and contexts, but the one thing it must contain is a fact-based quantification of the opportunity or the "size of the prize." In addition to establishing financial attractiveness, a fundamentally sound HBC also communicates to upper management and the organization as a whole that this effort is not a token effort. Rather, it is an obligation—a smart resource allocation backed up by compelling data. A solid HBC deconstructs the "size of the prize" and begins identifying the roadblocks to capture it at a high level. The HBC ties directly into the Hispanic performance tracking covered later in Chapter 7. In an environment where the amount of funds dedicated to Hispanic marketing is always in jeopardy, you should never rest on your laurels.

Consistently putting effort into understanding and communicating the value of marketing to Hispanics also means that an organization's HBC should ideally be updated annually as a part of the business planning cycle. An HBC that is two or three years old invites skepticism and potentially reinforces the notion that the Hispanic effort is not grounded in rigor. Keep in mind that the business case might need to be made at both the aggregate and brand levels, and also at the business unit level, making the imperative relevant to middle management.

During my stint at Miller Brewing, I was exposed to a best-in-class HBC that I think can serve as a model to other companies. The Miller HBC made sure to document obvious rationale points, like the growing population of Hispanics in the U.S., but it didn't stop there as it drilled down into more relevant, category-specific data. It also looked at lesser-discussed dynamics, including an analysis of how the beer consumption habits of Hispanics differ from habits of non-Hispanics. But the coup de grâce that frankly blew me away was that Hispanic consumers actually represented better profit margins and contributed a disproportionate share of industry profit margin. This disproportionate profitability was all based on the type of beer that Hispanics preferred and the proximity of breweries to key Hispanic markets. In other words, this particular HBC was fairly unique in terms of how nuanced it was, and it thus was uniquely effective at convincing its audience. Keep in mind that in some situations you might be establishing the HBC in order to run a pilot market test, which in turn will help you to later make a stronger business case to invest in the Hispanic market.

Components of a Hispanic Business Case

Here are the component parts I recommend be part of an HBC:
1. Set the stage: The first step should be to make clear to

your audience that Hispanic marketing constitutes a high-level opportunity. An easy way to start is with an overview of Hispanic demographics, like Hispanic population growth rates or their geographic concentration across the U.S. Make sure to focus on any key geographies that are relevant to your business. It is also essential to contrast these data points to their non-Hispanic analogs.

2. Establish category relevance: The second step is to drill down into your category-specific data and to contrast behaviors among Hispanics with those of non-Hispanics. This will help explain whether Hispanics are overdeveloped relative to the rest of the market (and you need to protect this franchise) or underdeveloped (you need to invest for growth).

3. Size the prize: The third step is to establish what Hispanics mean to your business today and what they can mean to it in the future. Because long-term vision here is so essential, this requires a series of well thought out assumptions. I highly recommend working on this task with anyone at your company that focuses on strategic planning.

4. Strategic alignment: I think it goes without saying, but it is tremendously helpful to highlight how the Hispanic effort supports a long-term business strategy. At Miller Brewing, there was actually a business case template, and one of the first questions in the template related to whether the initiative in question supported the company's five-year business strategy. Envisioning the future is especially important for Hispanic marketing, given that we know Hispanic marketing efforts are so prone to restructuring and new leadership whenever they lack a clear purpose.

5. Miscellaneous: Other important dimensions that you should consider including in the HBC include:
    - Specifics on the resources you are requesting.
    - How is your competition likely to respond?

- By what standards are you measuring success?
- At what point will you know that these efforts have been successful?
- Who will be held accountable for delivering this effort's results?
- What is the probability that this effort will be successful and why?

By equipping yourself with the necessary facts to advocate for the appropriate levels of investment spend, the HBC helps you play offense. Plus, the HBC can also help you play defense in some cases—when the Hispanic effort is under evaluation and faces potential funding cuts, it is imperative to have readily available data that can be leveraged in support of protecting that investment.

Investment vs. Expense

I often work with clients who are interested in capturing at least their "fair share" of the Hispanic market opportunity, a topic I'll discuss in more detail in Chapter 4. Each one of these clients is in a very different place when it comes to determining how much money and resources to invest in the Hispanic opportunity. One of my clients has been focused on these efforts for years and thus has a very direct and intuitive approach to funding their investment in Hispanic initiatives. They've made things as simple as dedicating a certain rate of investment per "Hispanic case" sold. Obviously, this is dependent on the ability to isolate sales made to Hispanic consumers, which is not always as easy as it sounds given that many companies lack the measurement precision to accurately identify sales made to Hispanic consumers. Another one of my clients is essentially overcompensating for their long absence from the Hispanic market and even admits to possibly overinvesting in the opportunity. A third company I work with, which is at just the beginning of their Hispanic journey, is still grappling with how to fund this new, strategic priority of theirs.

So, while there is considerable variability in how companies are funding their Hispanic marketing efforts, I'm going to focus on this common third scenario, which is riddled with ambiguity. As such, my point of view here is probably most relevant to those firms just embarking on their Hispanic marketing journeys, although I think that lessons here can have broader relevance for companies at many different stages of development. Here's a simple guiding principle that will inform the rest of this anecdote: the initial, foundational Hispanic work must be approached as an investment versus as an expense. In other words, companies need to approach these foundational Hispanic efforts the same way they would an R&D investment or a capital improvement. Simply put, these preliminary efforts are a well-informed bet that an investment made today in the Hispanic effort will yield a solid return or positive net present value down the road. This approach also implies that a certain amount of due diligence has gone into quantifying the opportunity and making the business case for this investment. No one in their right mind would go to a new product development meeting and petition for a substantial R&D investment without a fact-based business case to support why such an investment would be a fundamentally sound business decision in the longer term. Likewise, plants are not built and factory equipment is not bought without such due diligence on the front-end.

However, too many times the Hispanic effort, whether at this foundational stage or a more evolved stage, is not funded as an investment but is treated like any other marketing or business expense. As a result, Hispanic marketing becomes especially vulnerable to the budget cuts that come with a focus on making the quarterly numbers. Can you imagine if the same limiting mentality dictated whether a plant was built or whether an R&D

initiative received funds? "Oh, sorry Bob, you can only build the walls for your new plant this quarter, and we'll have to see how the numbers look next quarter to determine whether we can afford the roof." That sounds nonsensical, right?

But that is essentially what happens when it comes to investment in the Hispanic opportunity, which needs nurture and protection to eventually be financially lucrative. This is part of the reason why the Hispanic effort rarely ever gains longer-term traction, as too many companies lose motivation when a financial windfall isn't immediate and then only invest in fits and starts. One of my clients once referred to these efforts as amounting to "random acts of Hispanic marketing." Therein lies the inherent problem: this effort can't be successfully pursued in an ad hoc manner.

An inconsistent and expense-driven view of the Hispanic effort also ends up failing because it creates systemic fatigue within an organization. With each indiscriminate budget cut people start to read between the lines and begin to internalize that the company is not really serious about the Hispanic opportunity and is only offering a nominal commitment to Hispanic marketing. This in turn discourages broader advocacy across the organization and fuels that destructive, self-fulfilling cycle I discussed in Chapter 1. Is it then any surprise when the high performers in the organization don't want to become part of the Hispanic team? Is it any surprise when the core brand groups in the organization don't make Hispanic one of their top priorities? Is it any surprise to then see staffers on the Hispanic team take their foot off the gas, stop taking risks and go into self-preservation mode? Obviously, many things have to align for the Hispanic initiative to succeed, but no component is more important than generating marketplace momentum, which can only be achieved with consistent investment levels that come with playing the long game.

These companies have to be forced (easier said than done, by the way) to look in the proverbial mirror and decide if they are really serious about tapping into the Hispanic opportunity or not. They have to determine and declare whether investing in Hispanic marketing is a "must do" or simply a "nice to do." They have to decide whether Hispanics are a priority target or not. There is no middle ground here; it's yes or no. The constant fits and starts communicate broadly that the front end, due diligence simply has not been done. In some cases, it might also communicate that the Hispanic effort is really more about optics than a true commercial growth initiative.

So, now you're convinced that you don't want your company to succumb to this all-too-common cycle. What now? I vehemently believe that avoiding these pitfalls necessitates two straightforward tasks: one is learning to embrace a philosophy, and another is developing a simple, mathematically driven process.

Step 1: Embrace a philosophy

I recommend that companies start approaching the U.S. Hispanic market like they would any other emerging market or in the same manner as they nurture new products. Implicit in these analogies is that a decision to enter a new or emerging market is a decision that is made and sponsored by the executive leadership of a company. Proven multinationals don't enter new markets expecting them to pay out in year one or two, as they typically have a much longer and realistic time horizon. They understand that a certain amount of investment spending is required and thus don't apply the traditional ROI criteria immediately out of the starting gates. Emerging markets are treated differently because they represent long-term opportunities, which require conceptualizing costs as investments, rather than as expenses.

Step 2: Develop the process

Build the business case first, do it right, and let it inform investment decision-making. Too many times, when you get underneath the reasons for inconsistent and vulnerable investment levels in the Hispanic market, it can all be traced back to the lack of a clear, fact-based, business case. A fitting parallel is when a multinational company decides that a particular country represents an attractive new market. Successful multinationals don't approach promising new markets with reluctance, and they certainly don't invest in fits and starts. They perform the necessary due diligence and let the analytical rigor make a very clear case in terms of dimensionalizing the opportunity. Once that initial due diligence is complete, the proverbial case is closed and rarely is it ever fully reevaluated. But just as P&G and Unilever don't constantly reconsider their investment in Guatemala or Cambodia every year, companies truly committed to the U.S. Hispanic opportunity don't continuously debate whether they should be funding Hispanic marketing or not. These multinationals might update their respective business cases as new information becomes available, but they don't approach their investments in emerging markets with a binary on-or-off switch. A multi-year commitment is implicit.

I want to close by making an important and related point. Sometimes, as I noted in the beginning of this chapter, the pendulum can swing too far in the opposite direction, and companies can overinvest. This disproportionate and unmerited amount of support can be harmful to the Hispanic effort in the long run as well. Instead of suffering from the natural reluctance many senior executives have that stems from an insufficient fact base, some companies overcompensate and throw the kitchen sink at the Hispanic opportunity. I am against this approach since it invariably will come back to hurt the

Hispanic effort. Down the road, this overinvestment will be leveraged by skeptics as an argument against the Hispanic opportunity going forward. If so much money was devoted to an effort that was only moderately or mildly successful, why invest in Hispanic marketing at all? The reason I reference the other side of the coin is to emphasize that even under favorable conditions, in which a company's senior leaders understand the Hispanic opportunity, there still has to be transparency, accountability, and oversight. Framing Hispanic marketing as an investment should never be misconstrued as condoning free spending without clear guardrails. Investment spending requires an unwavering commitment alongside customized and clear expectations.

The Alienation Myth

Some myths die hard. I've been working in the Hispanic arena for decades, dating back to my days heading up Gatorade's multicultural effort in the early '90s. Back during those halcyon "Be Like Mike" days, I often encountered concerns from upper management regarding the potential unintended consequences of our multicultural marketing efforts on the so-called "general market." Back in 1993—hardly the age of enlightenment for Hispanic marketing efforts—it seemed like a valid concern to others, especially given that Gatorade was essentially just sticking its toe in the multicultural waters. Sure, we had enlisted the help of Michael Jordan, the greatest multiculturally-relevant spokesperson of all time, but back in those days, he was thought of as a mainstream marketing asset and not specifically for use by those of those of us on the multicultural side of the business. This finally changed when an extremely talented and persuasive creative director by the name of Lisa Llewellyn at the UniWorld Group eventually eroded our upper management's resistance and produced a TV spot targeting

African American consumers featuring Michael Jordan during his hiatus from the NBA and stint in MLB.

Fast forward to today, and I still hear the similar concerns from many of my blue chip clients: comments like "We have to make sure the Hispanic effort is integrated, but without *alienating our core*," or "We have to make sure this work does not end up *being polarizing*." In other words, there exist too many senior executives and marketers today that, without evidence, continue to believe in this "alienation myth." Essentially, this disproven theory assumes that a company will lose its hard earned, non-Hispanic consumers (aka the "core" consumer) if it pays too much attention to its Hispanic consumers. Too many marketers today still want to have their cake and eat it too; they want to grow their business by engaging with Hispanic consumers, but only if such efforts do not offend the imagined sensibilities of their non-Hispanic, white user base. Today, we face a very different market reality that a surprising number of marketers have been slow to grasp, accept, and internalize. The reality is grounded in two core and readily apparent truths:

Truth #1: The "general market" is no longer simply about white people, and your brand better catch up with the times, or it is going to be left behind. I'm not going to rehash all the data and trends other than to point out one very compelling statistic: in 2020, according to data from the U.S. Census Bureau, people of color represent 40.3 percent of the U.S. population, while Hispanics make up over 18 percent of the U.S. population.[3] These numbers are only increasing: people of color are expected to represent 44.2 percent of the U.S. by 2030, while Hispanics will account for over 21 percent. In other words, more than one out of every five Americans will be Hispanic by

---

[3] Ibid.

2030. Plus, non-Hispanic whites will eventually become a minority, dropping below 50 percent of the U.S. population around the year 2045.[4]

The rapidly, shifting demographics are even more compelling if you look at youth and the ten largest metros in the U.S. As of January 2020, non-Hispanic Caucasians under the age of 18 were already a minority among their age group. My firm completed a study a few years ago focused on Hispanics in California, and one statistic still resonates with me: 55 percent of California's public school population is Hispanic.[5] Let's face it: the brands that are most likely to hold on to this alienation myth are those that have a core user that is white working class and is more likely to live in a rural, racially homogenous area. But even brands catering to that demographic are already changing. The most prominent example is NASCAR, one of the most powerful brands in the country and one that has disproportionately relied on a white working-class fan base (many of whom proudly declare themselves "rednecks"). NASCAR has hardly suffered since first adding a prominent Hispanic driver, Juan Pablo Montoya, to its roster in 2006, and it is finding that Hispanics are increasingly drawn to the sport, as evidenced by the addition of other Hispanic drivers. A few years ago, my firm conducted some research in Charlotte, North Carolina, which is the epicenter of NASCAR culture. The study revealed two key findings:

1. The non-Hispanic NASCAR fan in Charlotte did not have any issues with NASCAR's push to become more relevant with Hispanics, and with Juan Pablo Montoya in particular.
2. The Hispanic consumer in Charlotte is surprisingly

---

[4] Ibid.
[5] California Department of Education, "Fingertip Facts on Education in California—CalEdFacts,"
https://www.cde.ca.gov/ds/sd/cb/ceffingertipfacts.asp.

aware and interested in NASCAR.

If NASCAR can cater to increasingly diverse segments of the population, so can every brand and so should every brand.

Truth #2: Not only do non-Hispanic whites make up an increasingly smaller portion of the population, they are also increasingly multicultural in their own sensibilities and values. Simply put, today's non-Hispanic white millennial is much more attuned to racial diversity and much more open-minded about different groups of people than their parents were. We need to put an end to this alienation myth once and for all.

What does this mean for how a company should approach its Hispanic and its non-Hispanic marketing efforts? Simply put, both efforts must flow from the same brand strategy, and both efforts must have the same tone, manner, and feel. Rather than wondering, "How do I avoid alienating my core consumer?" companies should instead be asking themselves, "How do I ensure that my total marketing efforts are inclusive of my multicultural audience?"

3

THE HISPANIC FUNCTIONAL PLAN

Once you have a compelling Hispanic Business Case in place (and prior to declaring a winning ambition for Hispanic efforts, which is discussed in Chapter 4), the THM discipline necessitates the development of a Hispanic Functional Plan (HFP). An HFP is a plan that describes how, when, and where the objectives and goals will be accomplished for the Hispanic function. Most marketers—let alone most Hispanic marketers—have never heard of a functional plan, but it is an intuitive next step in THM's capability building process. An HFP applies to all of the efforts marshalled against the Hispanic opportunity, whether delivered through a marketing team or more broadly within an organization.

Why You Need an HFP

So why does it matter and why is it necessary? You will recall from the Introduction that I recently worked with the head of the Hispanic effort at a very large, lapsed client. When we started working together on some planning deliverables for senior management, I asked him what his team's role and purpose were, as that would in

turn inform much of the planning process. I specifically asked him the following questions:
- Was his team exclusively focused on Hispanic insights, or was it also responsible for broader Hispanic strategy?
- Was his team responsible for uncovering brand-specific insights or insights at the category level?
- Similarly, would his plans include Hispanic strategies at the brand level or at the portfolio level?

These types of questions were necessary in order to better understand the how narrow or broad his functional responsibilities and imperative were. This type of granularity was necessary before embarking on a planning process and delineating specific activities that needed to be accomplished over the coming year. In short, the HFP should specify 1) what the Hispanic team actually owns, 2) what the team is ultimately accountable for, and 3) what interdependencies the team has. Think of the HFP as a job description for the entire Hispanic effort. The HFP is developed by the leader of the Hispanic marketing team and its target audience is both upper management and the broader commercial enterprise. It might be hard to believe, but many Hispanic marketing leaders are placed in their roles without clear guidance as to what they actually do and own.

Key Choices That Will Influence the HFP

There are many different ways to configure the Hispanic function, and there are a number of key dimensions that should influence these choices:
1. Hispanic Business Ownership: Will the Hispanic team own the Hispanic business strategy and have a profit & loss statement (even if it is a shadow P&L[6])? Does

true custodial responsibility exist? This is a significant determinant of the team's accountability and immediately establishes whether they are the true business owners.
2. Doers Versus Advisors: Will the Hispanic team produce actual marketing tools, or will it play more of an advisory and internal consulting role? This in turn can depend on the size and capacity of the team. One of my clients is currently a one-person team, which forces them into playing more of an advisory, subject matter expert role. This is a fairly common situation, especially when the Hispanic effort is still proving itself to upper management. In these situations, it is important to establish which combination of the following roles a one-person team will take on:
   a. *Evangelist* of the Hispanic strategy: Focused on the ongoing and methodical evangelization of the Hispanic strategy across the organization.
   b. *Enabler* of the Hispanic strategy: Focused on closing key gaps in the capability and ensuring it is actionable.
   c. *Enhancer* of the Hispanic strategy: Focused on developing marketing tools that complement the strategy.
   d. *Aligner* of the Hispanic strategy: Focused on ensuring that the broader enterprise is working in alignment (aka compliance) with the Hispanic strategy versus at odds with it.
3. Narrow Versus Broad Orientation: Is the Hispanic team focused on communications only? Or does it have a broader marketing purview, or maybe even a more holistic, commercial orientation?

An effective HFP delineates the outcomes of the above

---

[6] A shadow P&L is not the official P&L statement. It is one kept for internal purposes in order to track the performance of a particular cost center or business unit, based on allocated costs and revenues.

choices and in doing so further clarifies the role of the Hispanic team and function. This in turn reduces ambiguities across the organization, and sets up the Hispanic effort for greater success.

Components of an HFP

The HFP should include most, if not all, of the following components as it answers the following existential questions about the Hispanic effort:

1. **Functional Role**
- What is the Hispanic function's reason for being?
- What does the Hispanic function do that is unique from what everyone else at the company does?
- What distinct skills are required for the Hispanic function that no other function needs as deeply? How does this affect what the function does and doesn't do?

Clearly, a solid description of the role of the Hispanic function must explicitly reference the fact that the Hispanic function is uniquely tasked with capturing growth from the Hispanic market. This description will typically also emphasize a certain resident expertise that the Hispanic function can then make available to other parts of the organization.

Example of a functional role
If tasked with answering the question, "Why does this team exist?" the following illustrative statements provide solid examples:
- "The Hispanic market is critical to the future success of our company due to the Hispanic market's sheer size, rate of growth, and profitability."
- "Our traditional brand marketing approach is insufficient for the Hispanic market due to language

barriers, cultural nuances, and different media platforms."
- "We must chart the direction for the system (i.e., company, trade partners, and other entities involved in going to market) in terms of how to capture more than our fair share of growth from the Hispanic market."
- "We must help the system understand the business imperative that the Hispanic market represents (e.g., what the size of the prize is and why it is critical to overall success?)."
- "We must identify what it will take to win with Hispanic consumers."

If tasked with answering the question, "What does the Hispanic team do, exactly?" the following illustrative statements should provide solid examples:
- "We lead the organization across all corridors of the Hispanic imperative."
- "We create a comprehensive Hispanic Business Strategy across the value chain."
- "We develop and maintain a robust, actionable view of the Hispanic market that will inform the brand propositions, opportunity prioritization, and ultimately the strategies for growth."
- "We provide clear business guidance and set the strategic priorities for other major functions (e.g., sales, public relations, product development, etc.)."
- "We foster the right mindset across the organization and work to constantly reinforce it, in order to ensure a consistent view of Hispanic consumers across the company."
- "We facilitate the exchange of best practices and create a best-in-class capability."

If tasked with answering the questions, "What is unique

about the Hispanic team?" or "What does the Hispanic team do that no one else already does within the broader marketing department?" the following illustrative statements should provide solid examples:
- "We provide the system with subject matter expertise in terms of the Hispanic consumer and the retail community that serves them."
- "No other function within the marketing organization is focused on unacculturated and bicultural, Spanish-dominant Hispanics. Note: Our current strategy attacks the opportunity from both ends of the acculturation spectrum—Acculturated Hispanics are the domain of the [total market] brand teams."

2. Convictions and Resulting Mandate

This section of the HFP declares the strongly held beliefs required of the Hispanic function in order to support desired business performance and any transformation called for in the strategy. These underlying convictions provide the basis for mandates, or phrases that begin with "therefore we must...."

Example of a conviction and a resulting mandate:
"Our primary opportunity lies with bicultural and acculturated 21-34 year old Hispanic males, so *therefore we must* develop an engagement model that specifically targets that group's passion points."

3. Team Goals and Tangible Outputs

This section of the HFP forces the Hispanic team to clarify upfront what the Hispanic function is going to actually do in order to create value and deliver on its stated role. Many Hispanic teams I've worked with lack this discipline—a clear declaration of what it is that they are going to do and how such efforts support the broader mission of the marketing function and company. Statements fulfilling the purpose of this section should summarize the quality requirements and link to higher-level strategic goals.

Example of team goals and tangible outputs:
"Our sales to Hispanic consumers are expected to outpace those to non-Hispanics by 5 percent and increase our share gap versus our primary competitor."

4. Requirements for Success

The fourth core section in the HFP details what the Hispanic team needs in order to deliver on its plans. The value of this component part can't be overstated. Providing clear requirements for success from the onset holds the team accountable to its own goals, while also making clear to upper management that saddling the Hispanic team with far fewer resources than what the team initially asked for is a recipe for failure. When providing requirements for success, it's no time to be shy. Make clear what you need, in terms of:

- People
- Systems and processes
- Environment and culture
- Upper management commitment
- Measurement system capabilities

5. Strategic Trade-offs

This section of the HFP articulates what changes need to be made to the Hispanic effort based on careful consideration of the available capabilities and resources. This is an opportunity to explicitly declare which of the current team efforts will be discontinued or put on hold in the coming fiscal year, which will provide the team more resources to devote to essential efforts and can also help position the team to the broader organization as financially disciplined.

Examples of strategic trade-offs:

- "We will discontinue acquiring sponsorships that appeal primarily to acculturated Hispanic males."
- "We will renegotiate our agreement with Univision in order to allow for more media budget flexibility, as we are up against a rapidly changing competitive environment."

6. Requisite Skills Needed

This section of the HFP articulates what skills are needed within the Hispanic team in order to deliver on the role.

Examples of requisite skills needed:
- "In order to develop a true Hispanic capability, we require expertise in terms of what it takes to win with Hispanic consumers and retailers who serve them (e.g., independent small stores) and the distributors who serve them. Strategic marketing skills are essential."
- "A cultural acumen and fluency in Spanish are desirable, but not required skills."

Company Archetypes

The robustness and complexity of an organization's HFP will depend in large part on where it is in its Hispanic enlightenment journey. Thus, I want to spend some time reflecting on the wide range of Hispanic marketing efforts I have been exposed to over the years. Approaches have ranged from neglecting the segment entirely, to patronizing it with ethnocentric messages that often rely heavily on unfair out outdated stereotypes, and to more enlightened approaches. I segment the client universe into five archetypes and place them on a spectrum based on their mindset regarding the Hispanic opportunity. This also sets up the potential capability evolution that THM can generate:

Figure 3: Hispanic Mindset Spectrum

1. **The Deniers**: These are companies that simply resist the idea that the Hispanic market represents a viable opportunity for them. They rely on any one of several tired myths to ignore the opportunity and the need for a distinct strategy. Some of these excuses include:
   - "Hispanics don't buy our brands in any large numbers, so they are not important to our business." Obviously, this head-in-the-sand approach ignores what the potential opportunity might be and is often not grounded in facts. Rather than pursuing a rigorous opportunity assessment of this new potential market, this unsophisticated mindset relies primarily on assumptions.
   - "Hispanics behave like the general market and thus don't require a separate or dedicated effort." There are rare instances where this might hold true, but few of these companies have really done the due diligence to understand the points of convergence and divergence between the two groups.
   - Another head-in-the-sand rationale is the classic statement "We can't afford to do it," which suggests that a company has not conducted the due diligence to understand the cost-benefit trade-offs. It is unlikely that these types of firms have really done the work to understand and frame the opportunity but are simply making clear that the Hispanic market is not a priority.

   Implication: These types of companies are not ready to harness the power of an HFP.

2. **The Lazy**: This group includes companies that are not actively selling to Hispanic consumers, but they are coincidentally benefiting from the Hispanic marketplace. This category also includes companies that have acknowledged the potential opportunity of the Hispanic market but have instead opted to do very little to actually pursue the opportunity. What this often looks like in practice is a company handing the entire effort to a Hispanic ad agency. In turn, its Hispanic efforts often involve the simplistic adaptation of total market efforts. There is no in-house Hispanic strategy development or research. These companies typically see the Hispanic opportunity as something they are forced to do for political reasons but not a pursuit that offers them any considerable value beyond that obligation. Their foray into the space is more symbolic than anything and is not rooted in commerce or making money. Their ultimate goal is just to signal to some key constituency that "we are doing something," and their efforts are often nothing more than token gestures.

    Implication: These types of companies are not ready to harness the power of an HFP.

3. **The Repeaters**: These are well-intentioned companies who actually do "get it" when it comes to the vast potential of the Hispanic market, but are hampered by chronic internal dysfunction. They are constantly reengineering their operations, hiring new staffers who have little sense as to what went wrong with the previous efforts. These types of companies tend to see the light every two to three years and literally start from scratch over and over again, never really benefiting from consistency or institutional knowledge.

    Implication: These types of companies will benefit

considerably from an HFP.

4. **The Zealous**: These are companies who have recently seen the light and are eager to crack the code with Hispanics. These companies often have just added a Hispanic-savvy senior executive to their ranks. They don't know exactly where to start, but they know that they have to do something and do it quickly or their inaction will have an opportunity cost. These companies tend to have a sense of urgency and have a greater chance of success than the repeaters, which have similar goals but have a history of failing to actually produce effective Hispanic marketing.

   Implication: These types of companies will benefit considerably from an HFP.

5. **The Enlightened**: As you would imagine, these are the companies that truly understand the value of the Hispanic opportunity and have understood it for a while. Not surprisingly, these companies benefit from consistent results from the Hispanic market. They represent the gold standard and provide best practices for others to emulate. Unfortunately, they represent only a small minority of all companies.

   Implication: These types of companies are likely already deploying an HFP.

This mindset spectrum theoretically also applies to agencies, but the sad reality is that very few Hispanic agencies can be classified as having an enlightened mindset. Very few of them eschew the traditional cultural stereotypes or treat Hispanic Marketing as a science. Keep in mind that companies and agencies can shift fluidly across this spectrum, as leadership and commitment changes. I'm hoping that this book helps more of them move in the right direction on this spectrum and avoid regression, which is all too common.

4

MAPPING THE STARTING AND END POINTS

The Hispanic Destination
- Mapping the End Point -

A key strategic pillar of THM is establishing where management wants to take the Hispanic business and specifying the results that are sought. You can only develop an effective Hispanic business strategy if you have a clear destination in mind. Companies and brands that have successfully addressed the Hispanic opportunity didn't reach that status by accident. They developed and declared a "Hispanic Destination" in advance and worked toward it across all their efforts. As cliché as it might sound, if you don't know where you're going, there's very little chance you'll actually get there.

Businesses without a clear Hispanic Destination jump reactively from one Hispanic initiative to another without any consistent strategy functioning as the connective tissue. At most companies, this winning ambition for the Hispanic effort is often missing, which relegates most Hispanic efforts to mere tactics. In other words, without the guidance of a Hispanic Destination, the Hispanic effort often defaults to focusing on activities versus on outcomes. It's analogous to packing your bags for vacation without having first decided where you are actually going.

Destination planning was a concept that I was introduced to during my tenure at The Coca-Cola Company. The concept of a winning ambition as a guidepost is not a proprietary idea as it exists by many names in the business world and certainly applies more broadly than the Hispanic context. However, this type of strategic rigor is typically missing in the Hispanic marketing arena. If you want to go even deeper than the material I cover in this chapter, I highly recommend the book *Playing to Win: How Strategy Really Works* by A.G. Lafley and Roger L. Martin (no relation).

One of the benefits of the Hispanic Destination planning process is that it brings senior executives into the same room to hash out what the true end game is for the Hispanic effort. The Hispanic Destination work should be conducted at the corporate level first. Brand-specific Hispanic Destinations can also be helpful but should be crafted later and informed by the higher-level, corporate Hispanic Destination. These discussions are so important because too many companies fail to articulate clear business objectives for their Hispanic business. Reaching consensus on quantifiable objectives is the most important aspect of the Hispanic Destination and, not surprisingly, is also the part that is most difficult to reach consensus on. Many companies can cite the Hispanic consumer measures they want to achieve—like "brand awareness," for instance—but what is often missing are clear market share and profit objectives for this consumer segment. Seems intuitive enough, right? However, most companies have not articulated a corporate Hispanic Destination for two primary reasons:

1. The person in charge of the Hispanic function is too junior to make a case for this executive level activity.

2. As noted earlier, few companies have done the due diligence in the form of a solid business case (e.g., current state + quantified opportunity) to be able to articulate a coherent Hispanic Destination.

These are just the most common reasons I've evidenced, but many other factors can lead a Hispanic team to lack a clear destination. Many leaders of the Hispanic function haven't been exposed to the concept of a winning ambition, and for others, the process is perceived as too cumbersome. These situations are often accompanied by a floundering Hispanic effort that suffers from constant fits and starts. Hispanic destination planning is one of the hardest steps to undertake because there is a lot of consensus building that must take place up front. For it to really take hold, destination planning must take into consideration the perspectives of the entire executive team. This need for executive team consensus alone is enough to dissuade a lot of people from the pursuit entirely, as they might not feel comfortable taking this up the chain of command, especially in organizations where Hispanic marketing has been marginalized or misunderstood. Another common stumbling block is if the CMO doesn't feel compelled to involve other members of the C-suite and particularly the CEO as he or she sees it as the domain of marketing only. Hierarchy and optics often get in the way.

The Hispanic Destination is articulated in a "Hispanic Destination Declaration," which is a statement of what you hope to achieve in the context of the Hispanic opportunity with specifics about the actual results you covet from marketing to Hispanics. The Hispanic Destination Declaration clearly articulates what business model, results, and rewards a company seeks to achieve via the Hispanic business over the medium term. A clear declaration sets the foundational direction for all Hispanic activity in the company; it is a touchstone for all efforts.

But what should actually be included in such a declaration? Ultimately, an effective Hispanic Destination Declaration should:
- Aim high and be aspirational, while also being achievable.
  - Too much slack between the destination and the current state can result in lost credibility and poor morale.
  - While too little slack between the destination and the current state is likely to result in missed opportunity (underachievement).
- Be expressed in terms of the desired outcomes. It must detail what success looks like. For instance, it should include some, if not all, of the following:
  - Metrics in terms of financial performance.
  - Metrics in terms of market position and scale.
  - Metrics in terms of people and culture transformation.
- Have the specificity required to guide the decisions the company makes.
- Be grounded in convictions that are unassailable and consistently practiced.

The clearer the Hispanic Destination Declaration is, the greater the odds that the organization can actualize it and develop a Hispanic business plan that is achievable.

As previously mentioned, consensus is an essential part of the Hispanic destination planning process. A good way to bring stakeholders together and reach agreement is through a working session; at least one is needed, though more can be helpful depending on a company's specific needs. But who should participate in a Hispanic destination planning working session?
- The Hispanic leadership team, the owners of the Hispanic function, or both.
- Anyone who will be accountable for success of the

Hispanic function (e.g., so if the success of Hispanic marketing is a key performance indicator of the CMO or even the CEO, those leaders should be directly involved in crafting the declaration and participating in the corresponding work sessions).

Example of a Hispanic Destination Declaration:
"We will develop a systemic business capability toward the Hispanic market that is unparalleled in the consumer goods industry, achieving both strategic and operational excellence. Therefore, we will become a growth engine for our company by consistently exceeding our total revenue growth rate. As a result, we will consistently close the corporate share gap between us and our primary competitor."

The Hispanic Situation Assessment
- Mapping the Starting Point -

It's not enough to develop a clear sense of your desired future state as you must also develop a clear sense for your current state in order to identify the right strategies to close the gap between the two. This is accomplished through the development of a Hispanic Situation Assessment (HSA). The purpose of HSA is to develop an internal and external view of the current Hispanic business and identify opportunities for growth. It is an important due diligence exercise, and it can even precede the development of the Hispanic Destination if that sequence is preferable. The HSA provides another opportunity to align with company leaders about the critical issues facing the Hispanic business.

In terms of sequencing, Hispanic destination planning can precede the Hispanic Situation Assessment, or flow from it, but it should always be informed by the Hispanic Functional Plan. I prefer to conduct the Hispanic Situation Assessment after the destination planning work in order to focus the assessment on identifying the barriers that stand in the way of reaching the Hispanic Destination.

At a high level, the HSA should aim to answer the following strategic questions:
- What is the current state of the Hispanic business?
- What is working, what is not working, and why?
- What are the key barriers that will impede us from reaching the Hispanic Destination?
- What opportunities exist to grow your Hispanic business?
- What barriers & challenges need to be overcome?
- What do you need to learn?
- What are the priorities?

This last point is obviously the most important one. One way to facilitate productive discussion here would be to focus the four to five most important things a team should work on to grow the Hispanic business. These opportunities will determine which strategies & programs to pursue, and in turn will inform where the Hispanic team's time will be spent (and implicitly, where the team's time will not be spent).

The HSA development process typically includes the following component parts:
- **Assess Existing Hispanic Data**: In this step, you will work with any relevant existing Hispanic research to understand the operating context and challenges facing your company, and to also begin building hypotheses about opportunities to drive growth. A fresh set of eyes can typically extract new value from existing data, and a key focus should be on identifying areas of potential improvement. With this step, you should also identify key gaps in the information that need to be addressed via new research efforts, whether primary or syndicated. The scope of the HSA's information review obviously depends on the

priorities of the business and what information is available, but some areas I have focused on in the past include assessing the following (with a focus on dimensions that might impact consumer behavior):
- Consumer and category trends (Tip: It's important to de-average the data, so don't stay at the national level with your analyses—break things down further)
- Competitive information
- Geographic, consumer, and portfolio strategy dimensions
- Media spend and mix
- Positioning and integration with total market efforts (i.e., Hispanic expression of unified brand positioning)
- Informed hypotheses that inform the development of the learning agenda (so as to avoid "boiling the ocean" type research, which is too expansive)

- **Competitive Audit**: It is also important to conduct an audit with a focus on identifying what the competition's core Hispanic strategies are and what their brand activation platforms look like. If possible, you should also examine their commercial initiatives in order to identify broader advantages that they are exploiting.
- **Key Constituent Interviews**: I highly recommend interviewing key trade partners such as wholesalers and retailers. This is often an overlooked step, but it can yield tremendous insights. It is so important to look outside of your own organization and see things from the perspective of your trade partners. This key activity can often be complemented by retail audits since you are presumably already out in the marketplace.

There is a secondary benefit to conducting an HSA. An HSA can help address a significant pitfall I've called out in this book: that institutional knowledge is poorly archived and transferred as people rotate through roles. A solid HSA can serve as an important reference point for well beyond immediate Hispanic marketing efforts.

5

THE COMPLICATED ROLE OF CULTURE

What follows is a description of an actual call I was part of a number of years ago. I was invited to present the deliverables of the Hispanic segmentation work we had done for PepsiCo to the Mountain Dew brand team. This brand team's freshly-minted Hispanic agency was also asked to join the call to provide their point of view on acculturation. I was barely done presenting an overview of our engagement, which was grounded in the rigor of several thousand, in depth consumer surveys, when the overly eager agency account person began to chime in, as if elbowing into the conversation was the only way to prove his value to the client.

Ultimately, he effectively hijacked the meeting, spouting off a bunch of nonsense when his agency had been on board for all of one week. The first thing that struck me was that this agency guy had a surprisingly thick accent for someone we knew had been in the U.S. for a couple of decades, and this seemed to make everyone else at the meeting averse to challenging him—as if having an accent made him *more* Hispanic, or somehow *more* credible weighing in about Hispanic marketing. He began his monologue with "Hispanics love music," and followed up that little gem with, "We don't agree with your brand's major emphasis on the NFL, as we think it has to be complemented by soccer since Hispanics love soccer." Really? Hispanics love music and soccer! Who knew?

I could not believe what I was hearing. Here we were decades into the so-called "golden era of Hispanic marketing" and this guy, who represented a very well-established Hispanic ad agency, was imparting the gospel by telling a bunch of seemingly awestruck clients that Hispanics love music and soccer. It was on days like that one that I would find myself abruptly shifting from "I need to get out this business" to "I need to finish the damned book and call out some of the bull shit in this industry." Obviously, the latter finally won out. Now mind you that this mind-numbing, conference call had several ironies—one of the clients on the call was later slated to be a guest speaker at the Association of National Advertisers' (ANA) annual conference in Miami Beach. Yes, the same guy who hired this agency and seemed astounded by the revelatory link to soccer and music would end up sharing his own Hispanic pearls of wisdom to a packed house. Here are some of the other gems the Hispanic agency shared on the call:

- "Effectiveness and efficiency are both important when targeting Hispanic consumers." Yes, you heard it here first...you need BOTH effectiveness and efficiency!
- "Any focus on California and Texas requires a more unacculturated/bicultural emphasis." My jaw dropped when I heard this one, as if California and Texas were being overrun by less acculturated Hispanics while the more acculturated ones theoretically fled to other states. Any attempt to oversimplify the Hispanic demographics of Texas or California—or any state, for that matter—should be a dead giveaway that you are not dealing with a proven strategist.

- "High-level strategic pillars and passion points should guide your activation plans." This is a favorite cliché of many agencies, whether Hispanic or total market. Passion points drive everything. Whatever happened to brand strategy and letting that define activation?
- "Hispanics tend to be more image-driven consumers." So, Hispanics are more image driven or image conscious than non-Hispanics? Talk about a clichéd stereotype.
- "Unacculturated consumers of today are different from the unacculturated consumer 10 years ago. On the other hand, acculturation is not a linear process, and bicultural consumers are a stand-alone group who require Hispanic messaging (vs. Spanish messaging)." My head was starting to spin.
- "Culture is the new language!" I could discuss this one for hours if I really understood what the hell this guy was trying to say, but this was typical Hispanic agency jargon. Culture is the new language? As John McEnroe famously exclaimed, "You cannot be serious!"

The notion that Hispanic marketing equals cultural marketing is incredibly pervasive in our industry. I recently visited the website of an experienced consultant I know who specializes in Hispanic marketing. At the end of his bio, he listed the following motto as a summary of his professional philosophy: "Culture trumps strategy any day of the week."

Culture Should Not Influence Strategy

I agree that Hispanic culture has a role to play when marketing to Hispanics as it can certainly be relevant in the creation of messaging and programs, but I am also convinced that culture should not form the basis for marketing strategy. The faulty belief that all we have to do to connect with Hispanic consumers is activate some link to culture—whether it's a celebrity, a holiday, or a type of music—is one of the most prevalent myths promoted in the Hispanic advertising industry. Ultimately, an overemphasis on culture leads to subpar marketing. I was surfing through my Twitter feed one recent evening and came across a promoted tweet from Coca-Cola Racing that read: "In celebration of #HispanicHeritageMonth and inspired by @daniel_suarezg's roots in Monterrey, Mexico, the No. 96 paint scheme features bright, bold colors and textures from traditional Saltillo sarapes. See it on the track this weekend at #BofAROVAL. #HHM2020."

Coca-Cola Racing followed up this tweet a few days later with the following: "In need of delicious inspiration for your race day fare? You've come to the right place! Tweet to unlock @daniel_suarezg's Two Handed Tacos recipe."

I immediately realized that these two tweets would help reinforce one of the points I am trying to make in this book. While I think Coca-Cola's tweets and association with Daniel Suarez are well intentioned, this is yet another example of cultural marketing…just add bright, bold colors, a reference to Saltillo sarapes and a taco recipe and it is "mission accomplished"— Hispanic consumers will flock to brand Coca-Cola for its acknowledgement of Mexican culture. It's not that easy.

Activating cultural cues in marketing executions does not replace the need to intimately understand your Hispanic target as a consumer, but too many marketers think vague and undifferentiated nods to culture are all they need to do. On the contrary, marketers should treat Hispanics just like any other target consumer group, and as such, should focus on:

- **Segmentation**: In order to segment the addressable universe and identify the Hispanic segments that represent the most promising opportunities for your brand.
- **Targeting**: In order to profile the most attractive

Hispanic segments for your brand.

- **Positioning**: In order to understand what is most important to your target consumer and to, in turn, build a winning proposition based on those needs.

A few years back, my firm completed a Hispanic marketing strategy engagement for AutoZone, which is one of the country's leading auto parts retailers. Our findings were based on surveying over 750 Hispanic auto parts consumers, and in the end, we did not make a single culture-based recommendation. Instead, the research revealed which attributes were especially important to Hispanic auto part consumers, relative to their non-Hispanic counterparts——namely, the importance of things such as product warranties, the proximity of stores to Hispanic neighborhoods, and good prices. Our work then went a step further and identified how our client was performing on the most important attributes to Hispanic consumers: was the company performing better, worse, or about the same as its competition? These initial insights then provided a roadmap for the Hispanic marketing plan, making clear what AutoZone needed to keep doing, stop doing, and start doing. Culture had nothing to do with it, but marketing science did.

Culture Can Influence Advertising

The ad agency Third Ear—formerly known as LatinWorks—has been named the multicultural agency of the year by *Ad Age* multiple times and has won many Cannes Lions Awards over the past decade. As opposed to many other Hispanic ad agencies that continue to rely on stereotypical cultural cues and icons, Third Ear understands Hispanic consumers more deeply and has been at the forefront of this more nuanced way of thinking. This is not to say that Third Ear doesn't weave cultural insights into their creative work; they clearly do and to great acclaim. However, their co-founder and CMO, Alejandro Ruelas, will quickly point out that the underlying communication strategy they develop for clients is not conceived from culture, but rather from fact-based, strategic analysis.

The Emerging Market Analogy

A former colleague of mine used to invoke a poignant example of why companies should not develop marketing strategy based on culture. He used to point to the efforts made by some of the leading marketing companies in the world, like Nestlé or P&G when they market in emerging markets like Mexico. He would also point to how savvy, in-country marketers like América Móvil, the leading cell phone company in Latin America, market their brands and services in Latin America. These companies never relied on cultural stereotypes and instead activated their brands' unique selling propositions.

Why do so many companies that are marketing to Hispanics in the U.S. take such a different approach from Latin American companies marketing to their consumers? Do Hispanics become inalterably different the second they cross the border into America? Do U.S. Hispanics require a significantly different engagement model? I believe that the established players in our industry—namely, Hispanic ad agencies—have propagated the "myth of culture" for one very obvious reason: it has helped them sell Spanish-language ads. Keep in mind that I am not talking about millions of dollars here; I am talking about billions! Advertisers and marketers have bought into this myth hook, line, and sinker.

Culture Is Not Proprietary

Another compelling reason to shun culture as a cornerstone of marketing strategy is that culture is not proprietary. In other words, it can't be claimed by one brand at the expense of another. Sponsoring Maluma's next concert tour might seem like a surefire way to engage Hispanics, until you remember that such an event would sell multiple sponsorships across many companies. Or perhaps, your brand could sign Maluma, prompting one of your competitors to sign an equally popular Latin artist. Where does that leave you? Leveraging any one aspect of culture can be readily copied by the competition, who could easily learn from your company's mistakes and even improve upon your marketing.

An understanding of how culture impacts decision making within a particular product category can help avoid problems later. When I started working with Miller Brewing a number of years ago, I was surprised to find that they had been touting that Miller Lite was low in carbs to the Hispanic market. Mind you this low carb claim had been a huge hit among the total market as it was squarely on trend and represented a salient brand truth. The Hispanic team at the time had either been asleep at the wheel or had no influence within the organization because simply reiterating this low carb claim in Spanish to their unacculturated Hispanic target audience seemed a bit lazy to me. Intuitively communicating the low carb claim to Hispanics did not make sense to me, but since I don't claim to be a cultural expert, we conducted consumer research, which confirmed my suspicions and revealed that carbohydrates were irrelevant to unacculturated Hispanic males when choosing a brand of beer. They cared much more about fitting in, the badge value of the beer (i.e., the statement the brand makes about the drinker to other people that see them holding or consuming that brand), and whether they could drink several beers without losing control. The lesson is that culture should be scientifically, not anecdotally, understood in context.

While we are on the topic of Miller Lite, I want to share another example of when the brand mistakenly equated

Hispanic marketing with cultural marketing. At the suggestion of their ad agency, the Bravo Group, the previous Hispanic brand team at Miller Brewing had created a TV commercial geared to unacculturated Hispanic males featuring Alejandra Guzman, the popular, Grammy Award–winning Mexican singer and actress. At the time, she had a dedicated fan base throughout Latin America dating back to the late 1980s, and was known as "La Reina del Rock," or the "Queen of Rock" in the Hispanic world. There is no denying that she was a big deal in Hispanic popular culture. However, the choice to deploy her in Hispanic marketing provides a classic example of trying to leverage a cultural icon or cue when nothing else is working. Ad testing revealed that the TV commercial featuring Guzman did not drive sales among the Hispanic target consumer. At the same time, the brand's primary competitor, Bud Light, was deploying a host of other cultural icons in its Hispanic marketing mix, but had been more successful in its efforts since its marketing had a more intentional and clearer brand strategy. Another lesson learned: you can't culturally market your way out of a strategic problem like having an unclear and undifferentiated brand positioning. And relying solely on cultural cues can actually be counterproductive, by distracting from more essential marketing efforts.

Again, I'm not saying that culture is unimportant to Hispanic marketing, just that it has to be deployed cautiously and strategically. A total ignorance about Hispanic culture is another frequent misstep, one that I've encountered many times over my professional career. Two years ago, one of the leading African-American ad agencies in the country, UniWorld Group, reached out to me. They had just signed a new Fortune 100 client and their new client was having a difficult time simultaneously onboarding a new Hispanic agency due to some temporary contractual obstacles. My agency friends proactively saw an interim opportunity to fill a broader multicultural role, but they did not have anyone in-house that would fit the bill in terms of Hispanic marketing expertise. I represented a mercenary-like solution that could effectively act as this agency's Hispanic arm on an interim basis, while the client sorted out the contractual issues with their new Hispanic agency.

My first assignment presented itself quickly, and I was asked to book a flight to Los Angeles to observe a series of focus groups and then to provide a real-time, Hispanic point of view in the observation room and then again in subsequent debriefs. As it turned out, the focus groups were being used to gauge consumers' reactions to an extensive print ad campaign that had been developed by the client's longstanding agency of record (AOR)—and when I say longstanding, I mean 65 years! The client had astutely identified that its AOR lacked a strong multicultural acumen and had thus tasked it with "playing nice in the sandbox" with the new multicultural shops they had hired. This assignment turned out to be very insightful in terms of the blind spots large, total market agencies tend to have when it comes to the role of culture in engaging consumers of color. In a subsequent meeting at the client's headquarters, I took part in an extended debrief about the AOR's print campaign and its cultural relevance to Hispanics. It was pretty easy to spot some of the AOR's cultural miscues:

- For starters, the print campaign was entirely focused on the theme of freedom and depicted a number of people on motorcycles traversing the wide-open spaces we associate with the rural, southwestern U.S. The only problem was that the client's Hispanic consumer was not interested in that type of freedom or the escape that comes with jumping on a motorcycle and hitting the open road. Previous research had revealed that the Hispanic consumers the company was targeting instead wanted to focus on work in order to make a better life for themselves and their families. The Hispanic consumer was more interested in ambition than aspiration and escape. We even heard a consumer in one of the focus groups explicitly state, "I am not looking for adventure."

- Many of the print executions featured people doing fairly risky things, again in service of the brand's freedom ethos, like popping a wheelie on a motorcycle. Many of the Hispanic focus group respondents labeled these images as too risky. I advised the AOR that "boldness" should be brought to life in a culturally relevant manner; it can't be rebellious or reckless.
- I also vocalized to the AOR my concern about their use of stereotypical images to depict Hispanic consumers. Several of their print executions depicted Hispanic actors performing auto maintenance on lowriders. I still remember a respondent in one of the focus groups sharing, "That is what *cholos* do versus what I'm into." While I explained to the AOR that many Hispanic consumers appreciate manual labor and the art of the craft, such imagery was stereotypical.
- Lastly, I kept hearing the AOR make references to the "urban consumer." I explained that this concept is a marketer's paradigm that does not translate effectively to Hispanic consumers, as I have yet to meet a Hispanic consumer that refers to him- or herself as being "urban." It might be time for the marketing industry to drop this term altogether.

At the end of the day, it was clear that this very large, mainstream ad agency did not understand how to create advertising that would resonate with Hispanic consumers. This experience also provided a lesson that Hispanic ad agencies and larger, non-Hispanic agencies misunderstand culture in different ways. The larger companies don't have enough specialized knowledge of Hispanic culture to deploy it successfully, while Hispanic ad agencies are often too quick to leverage culture when weightier questions about brand strategy should be priorities instead.

Culture Can Help You Profile

I recognize that the term "profile" comes with a certain amount of baggage, but what I am referring to here is a set of attributes that help you better define and describe a particular consumer segment. In this context, this is nothing more than a research term that relates to descriptive information. A few years ago, my firm developed a Hispanic segmentation for a large client that incorporated an array of cultural identification questions and statements, such as:

- What culture do you identify most with? U.S. culture or Mexican culture?
- At some point, I am planning on returning to Mexico to live or retire.
- I would never purchase products from a company that supports strict immigration laws.

These cultural identification statements helped us better define and separate the Hispanic consumer segments in a segmentation framework. For example, we identified two different segments of the adult Hispanic population who held significantly different attitudes and beliefs. We called one of the segments the "Loyalistas," who were more likely to agree that "The U.S. is my home country." The other principal segment, which we called the "Real Mexicanos," were much more likely to agree with statements like "I love everything about Mexico."

6

IT TAKES MORE THAN MARKETING

One of the key principles of THM is that you have a better chance of succeeding if you deploy more than just marketing. Instead, THM espouses a commercial orientation, a more holistic approach that activates other functions across the business, but especially sales and account management given the importance of access to the Hispanic consumer.

Demand Creation and Demand Fulfillment

This broader orientation acknowledges that in order to effectively address the Hispanic opportunity, you must focus on both demand creation efforts—the proverbial "pull" activities such as advertising meant to "pull" consumers toward your brand—and demand fulfillment efforts—the "push" activities such as making sure store shelves are actually stocked with your products. The demand fulfillment side of this equation should involve developing a winning service model for retailers who serve your target Hispanic consumers. A narrow-minded focus on the function of marketing is often ingrained in marketing organizations and is thus a very difficult barrier to overcome. In my opinion, this rigid paradigm represents one of the biggest impediments to developing a more effective and durable Hispanic capability.

Effective demand fulfillment typically will have implications for organizational design and resourcing, which add to the inertia. Not until my eye-opening stint at Miller Brewing did I fully understand this concept, as for years prior, I, too, had simplistically equated Hispanic efforts with Hispanic marketing. After all, when I was responsible for multicultural marketing at Gatorade, I exclusively focused on marketing and mostly advertising. The problem with focusing only on marketing is that if all you do is worry about creating demand via advertising and promotions, but you don't support these efforts with reciprocal demand fulfillment, you will have effectively wasted those demand creation dollars. For example, if you spend a certain amount of money on advertising to your Hispanic target, but your brand is not readily available in the stores they shop at, you've only created, but not fulfilled demand. Admittedly, every situation doesn't call for a robust commercial orientation, but it's important to start somewhere. In some cases, the effort to think beyond marketing needs to start out modestly as with the simple decision to add a Spanish-speaking customer service representative at one of your call centers.

Getting Local

THM also requires a shift from thinking of Hispanic marketing as an effort that takes place on a national level to efforts that can also materialize on a more local level. Integration and coordination across both levels is essential. The battle is often won or lost within individual communities and/or at the store level.

All this was made clear to me during my time at Miller Brewing. Upon joining that team, I inherited a fundamentally sound Hispanic business strategy, only to find out that the team was neglecting to sufficiently consider demand fulfillment. Prior to my arrival, the company had invested significant resources in the development of a strategic sales force (SSF) focused on a group of pilot markets. So, what was this strategic sales force, and why did it exist? The SSF effort was essentially the brewery's attempt to compensate for a distributor network that it saw as not doing enough to address the Hispanic opportunity. The strategic sales force had been well-designed and in theory was supposed to act as a hybrid capability with a fairly broad mandate that included:

- **Sales**: Call on small, independent stores and develop long-term relationships with these critically important retailers that were serving the target Hispanic consumer.
- **Local Marketing**: Develop local Hispanic programs.
- **Community Relations**: Develop relationships with local Hispanic community groups.
- **Distributor Alignment**: Coauthor plans at the local level with key distributors in an effort to influence distributor behavior in terms of the Hispanic service package.
- **Retail Standards**: Must establish and execute against Hispanic store retail standards.

The SSF team had to do all of this while simultaneously providing feedback and sharing best practices with headquarters.

Upon joining Miller Brewing in my interim leadership role, I made an orientation visit to Texas to better understand the genesis behind the SSF and why distributors were supposedly failing to meet the needs of Hispanic consumers and the retailers who served them. As I crisscrossed the state and met with distributor leadership, two significant findings became readily apparent that I had not read in any of the many background documents I had inherited:

1. For starters, these distributors did not have a "Hispanic problem" at all. Keep in mind that unlike the constant turnover you would see at headquarters, these were family-owned businesses that had maintained a constant presence in their communities for generations. A distributor in Houston, Dallas, Austin, or San Antonio needed no explanation of the Hispanic business case. The script that I had prepared for these local market visits quickly became irrelevant. These distributors understood the importance of the Hispanic consumer better than anyone at headquarters. The quandary resulted from other brand assets that were working quite well with their Hispanic consumers—namely their distribution rights to a brand by the name of Corona Extra and it's smaller sibling (at the time) called Modelo Especial (ironically, Modelo Especial recently became the third largest beer in the U.S., eclipsing Coors Light). As it turned out, many of these distributors were making almost as much money selling these very popular, Mexican imports as they were the brewery's established, domestic brands. The distributors did not think they had a Hispanic problem…they believed the brewery did, and for the most part they were right. The irony was that all of these distributors had these really large Miller trademark signs on the front of their buildings that for years had been a big part of their identities. Yet if you really peeled the proverbial onion back you could make the argument that the sign on the front of the building should instead feature the Corona Extra trademark.
2. Distributor economics are predicated on volume. Any company involved in the delivery of goods makes more money when it delivers in bulk than when it delivers in labor-intensive, small batches. Thus, these beer distributors understandably tended to prioritize deliveries they made to large grocery stores like Kroger

and H-E-B over deliveries to the small, independently owned convenience stores that dominated high-density, Hispanic neighborhoods. In other words, the brewery and these distributors had priorities and business models that were not exactly in harmonious alignment. Hence, that disconnect justified the brewery's efforts to supplement local Hispanic efforts with the strategic sales force.

So, the SSF experience was my first practical exposure to how you can't simply market or advertise your way to success in the Hispanic arena. All of the Hispanic advertising funds that Miller Brewing was spending in Texas had a very limited return on investment since the distributor network was understandably prioritizing Corona Extra and large, chain stores.

During this same "wake up and smell the roses" road trip, I encountered another important lesson that highlighted how Hispanic demand creation efforts and demand fulfillment efforts are sometimes not aligned. Fortunately, my due diligence involved meeting with frontline personnel at the distributors and then with independent retailers. It took me a while to figure it out, but I eventually learned that one of the large Miller distributors was only delivering to independent, small stores in Hispanic neighborhoods on Fridays. This might not seem like a catastrophic decision, but as it turned out, in these types of stores, most beer is sold to Hispanic consumers on Friday afternoon and evening. The local Anheuser-Busch distributor, Silver Eagle, which at the time was thought to be one of the strongest distributors in the Anheuser-Busch system, was intentionally delivering to these same stores on Thursday morning. These stores typically only transacted with their customers and vendors with cash, so by the time they had bought a tremendous amount of Bud Light on Thursday, they had little money left. So, when Miller's local distributor stopped by on

Friday morning, the retailer almost always had little appetite for more domestic light beer and had little cash on hand anyway, and thus only made modest purchases.

Ultimately, a simple decision about the day of the week dramatically affected a Hispanic consumer's beer options and purchase decisions. So, when a Hispanic consumer walked into that store on Friday afternoon and was ready to buy their beer for the weekend (the critical end of week stock up occasion), what did they see? Back then it was referred to as the "wall of blue"—most cooler doors were full of the iconic blue packaging of Bud Light. This in turn was very effective in reinforcing the perception of leadership that is all too important to a segment of Hispanic consumers.

Anheuser-Busch was winning with Hispanics not because it necessarily had a superior product, and not because it was deploying breakthrough advertising or promotions. Anheuser-Busch was winning this particular battle because it understood that winning required a commercial effort, one that also paid close attention to the nuances of demand fulfillment.

Sadly, I discovered one last thing on my road trip through Texas. In the absence of a vigilant and connected Hispanic business leader at headquarters, most of the SSFs had been reassigned by the local market sales leader (given a dual reporting relationship) and were no longer performing their Hispanic-specific duties. Another valuable lesson learned, which had little to do with my traditional and rather narrow view of Hispanic marketing. This entire experience really challenged my views as a classically trained marketer who, at the time, tended to think that marketing was the center of the business universe or the "hub of the wheel," as we liked to refer to it. As marketers we can be quite arrogant in that tendency to think every problem can be solved through marketing or advertising. After all, when you only have a hammer, everything looks like a nail.

Amazon

I had to look no further than the titan of ecommerce for an example of how addressing the Hispanic market should involve business levers beyond advertising, especially as it relates to access. For context, Amazon was founded in Bellevue, Washington on July 5th, 1994, and its first products were shipped in 1995. However, it took Amazon over twenty years to add the Spanish language to its U.S. website. Until 2017, Amazon had imposed one implicit condition upon consumers in order to use its U.S. website: you had to know English. While you can make the case that it was better late than never, you can also ask, "Why did it take them so long?" It's worth noting that smaller Amazon stores in different countries had already offered a multiple-language experience. An Amazon shopper in Germany, for instance, could choose to shop in one of five languages: German, English, Dutch, Polish, or Turkish. For perspective, the Turkish speaking population of Germany at the time was under three million people. In contrast, the U.S. at the time had 42 million people with a mastery of Spanish, boasting more Spanish-speakers than most Latin American countries and only trailing Mexico, Colombia, Spain, and Argentina. Amazon's very cautious introduction of Spanish on its flagship U.S. site always struck me as a bit odd given their well-documented passion for customer obsession. After all, the best known of Amazon's 14 leadership principles makes clear that "Customer Obsession: Leaders start with the customer and work backwards. They work vigorously to earn and keep customer trust. Although leaders pay attention to competitors, they obsess over customers."[7]

---

[7] Amazon, "Leadership Principles," https://www.amazon.jobs/en/principles.

Clearly the powers that be at Amazon deliberated for a long time over a thorough analysis of the opportunities, threats, and unintended consequences (perhaps senior leaders held onto the alienation myth I discussed in Chapter 2). But, regardless, it is self-evident from the many years of delay that Amazon was hardly "obsessed" with the U.S. Hispanic consumer who preferred or needed to transact in Spanish. When first introduced, the effort certainly had its external critics as there were plenty of people who raised questions about the business acumen of adding the Spanish language to the site. These critics used arguments such as the fact that the vast majority of younger, native-born Hispanics speak only English at home or that about a third of all Hispanics speak both English and Spanish at home.[8] One additional data point: Amazon did not have full Spanish language support for Alexa devices until 2019 despite the fact that Amazon's digital assistant was already available in Spanish in Mexico and Spain. Thus, I would argue that Amazon has been late in deploying a more holistic orientation to the Hispanic market. Then again, you could make the argument that their competition has been even more delinquent. Nonetheless, Amazon's slow adoption of a Spanish-language U.S. site serves to make the case that even the most celebrated companies, even companies employing marketers with a keen understanding of the total market, are sometimes challenged in terms of how they address the Hispanic opportunity.

---

[8] Jens Manuel Krogstad, Renee Stepler, and Mark Hugo Lopez, "English Proficiency on the Rise Among Latinos: U.S. Born Driving Language Changes," Pew Research Center, May 12, 2015, https://www.pewresearch.org/hispanic/2015/05/12/english-proficiency-on-the-rise-among-latinos/.

7

HISPANIC PERFORMANCE TRACKING

Hispanic marketing is generally not a priority at the highest levels of many organizations, and it is rarely an explicit part of the CEO's agenda. This is often because the C-suite doesn't understand the incremental profit contribution that the Hispanic market can yield; in other words, the business case is missing. Even among many companies that do have a focus on the Hispanic market, the measurement systems they utilize are often not up to the task. Since many businesses can't isolate the sales they get from Hispanic consumers, they make an educated guess, which ultimately doesn't serve the effort well. The old adage, "You can't manage what you can't measure," is especially appropriate here.

Although measurement is an essential part of any business, the systems that are typically in place to measure the Hispanic effort are often not commensurate with how other parts of the business track their performance. It's as if the Hispanic business has been given a pass in terms of measurement rigor. This lack of consistency within an organization then helps perpetuate perceptions within a company that the Hispanic team isn't doing essential work. It's hard for upper management and the rest of the organization to see the Hispanic effort as truly legitimate if the right measurement systems aren't in place to drive transparency and accountability.

Measuring the performance of your Hispanic business ultimately comes down to one simple concept that in practice is often surprisingly difficult to pull off: At a minimum, you *must* find a way to isolate and track Hispanic sales and then to compare them to non-Hispanic sales. After all, it is very important to understand whether the Hispanic efforts are doing better or worse than non-Hispanic efforts. Ideally you also want to measure your Hispanic efforts against those of the competition. Your Hispanic efforts might seem successful, if looked at only relative to non-Hispanic marketing efforts, but a look at your competitors could reveal opportunities for further growth. This foundational element is surprisingly elusive even for some of the largest companies.

Building the System

Investing to build an effective Hispanic Performance Tracking (HPT) system is essential; nothing is more critical to the long-term viability of a Hispanic effort. It is important to note that I am not simply referring to a measurement system; instead, I am advocating for a system that uses measurements but establishes "performance" as a priority. A solid HPT system creates the context for the business plan. Here, too, I've observed an evolutionary process across clients, as an HPT system can initially function as just a reporting tool, but it can over time evolve into a performance management tool in service of the Hispanic business by holding the broader organization accountable.

Starting With Key Performance Indicators

The first step to developing any HPT System is to outline the key performance indicators (KPIs) that are going to be tracked. The second step involves building a system and capability to actually track them. The KPIs are often a combination of financial metrics, which track sales; attitudinal metrics, which track perceptions towards a category as well as specific brands; and behavioral metrics, which track things such as brand trial and repeat rates. Setting these Hispanic KPIs is fairly straightforward but is also dependent upon a number of factors, including constituent needs and budgetary parameters. It is important early in the process to make sure that the Hispanic KPIs are vetted, understood, and given the appropriate visibility across key constituencies.

Measurement Scope

Hispanic business performance is typically tracked at the aggregate level through traditional, measured channels like supermarkets. One of my current clients is currently only tracking supermarket data despite the fact that a disproportionate amount of Hispanic sales in my client's category is actually found elsewhere and flows through other measured channels as well as unmeasured channels, like independent convenience stores, bodegas, and regional Hispanic grocers. Don't get me wrong: something is always better than nothing, and supermarket-specific data is a solid starting point for many consumer products. However, this narrow scope often results in unintended consequences.

The problem often arises when the organization starts thinking that it has met the burden of proof from such a narrow stream of data and then takes its foot off the gas in terms of broadening the sources of their retail data. THM recommends that Hispanic business performance be tracked at the aggregate level and at the appropriate market level (e.g., designated market area), through measured channels like supermarkets and through nontraditional, unmeasured channels like bodegas. The system should be able to measure activity and performance at all levels (e.g., company, brand, key geographies) that an organization intends to influence. This should be the case because Hispanic KPIs should provide key intelligence about the operating entity, brand, and market levels. Clearly the measurement and accountability systems should be closely tied and should be informed by the Hispanic targeting strategy. For example, there is no point in measuring performance in bodegas if your Hispanic target is acculturated and does little shopping at such shops. Similarly, there is no point in measuring sales through supermarket chains like H-E-B or Safeway if your target Hispanic consumer doesn't shop there much. Setting up an effective HPT system requires an often-tedious focus on granular levels of data, often provokes disagreement within an organization, and can ultimately be quite expensive, especially if the KPIs are too broad and not oriented around a tight Hispanic target.

Developing an HPT System

I now want to spend some time discussing the key characteristics any successful HPT should include:

- It must align with the strategy: The HPT must reflect the strategic priorities of the Hispanic business.
- It must be coherent and focused: The HPT must track only those measures that are most critical to the success of the Hispanic strategy.
- It must integrate both internal and external measures: Businesses don't operate in a vacuum, and neither can your Hispanic metrics. You must tap both marketing information (data about the internal environment) and marketing intelligence (data about the external

environment).
- It must also be forward-looking: The HPT must investigate both lagging and leading indicators. An ideal system must serve as both a dashboard and a diagnostic tool.
- It must serve all constituencies: The HPT should include both a top-level snapshot and a disaggregated view of the business by brand, geography, consumer type, etc.
- It must be action-oriented: The HPT must take real time data and convert it into information that clarifies what you need to do.

In my experience, 12 months are typically required to design, internally test, and create a robust HPT system. However, actual development time is dependent upon business needs, current enterprise capabilities, and what modifications have to be made along the way. Timing projections should allow for iterative reviews of the utility and refinement of the measurement system by its champion and stakeholders. I typically approach the development process as follows:

- **Phase 1**: Conduct a Needs Assessment
  Determine your constituents' Hispanic business information needs for managing the business on a focus market basis and create an information architecture that summarizes these needs.
  o Deliverable: *Hispanic Information Architecture*

- **Phase 2**: Inventory the Current Reality
  Inventory the information currently available to manage the Hispanic business and identify the information gaps that exist based upon the Hispanic Information Architecture.
  o Deliverable: *Hispanic Information Inventory*

- **Phase 3**: Develop Templates
  Develop "strawman" templates that clearly define the information that the constituents need to run the business in the manner in which it should be presented, and populate these templates with all the information that is currently available.
  o   Deliverable: *Hispanic Strawman Templates*

- **Phase 4**: Develop the Plan
  Outline an implementation plan for closing the identified information gaps.
  o   Deliverable: *Implementation Plan*

Data Integrity

I now want to discuss the importance of getting underneath the data and ensuring that no methodology issues lead to misleading, incomplete, or ineffective Hispanic data. On one memorable engagement for a large consumer products company, my firm discovered several fundamental data integrity and methodology issues that were compromising the underlying quality of the client's HPT system:

First Issue: We identified that their legacy research suppliers were not providing a representative sample of Hispanic consumers in a number of critical ways:
- Acculturation: Unacculturated consumers—this was the client's Hispanic target consumer at the time—were considerably underrepresented in the sample because the legacy rescarch suppliers' mechanism for gathering data relied on phone interviews. Compounding this problem was that the legacy research suppliers' questionnaire and reports lacked a model that was predictive of the adoption of culture (acculturation) and thus did not capture the full acculturation spectrum. One supplier was using just

one question (the language selected by the respondent to take the survey) as a simplistic proxy for acculturation, while another supplier was also using just one question inquiring about the respondent's country of origin. On top of all that, the first supplier was using a binary unacculturated-acculturated designation—as if bicultural Hispanics simply didn't exist! In short, it didn't take long to figure out that this was a total mess, but there's more...

- Country of Origin: Hispanics of Mexican descent were being undercounted at the market level, as the data was not in line with U.S. Census Bureau data.
- Gender: Women were overrepresented in the total Hispanic sample too, skewing results. While 70 percent of my client's consumers were male, as much as 45 percent of the sample were women.
- Age: Varied dramatically by quarterly reporting period. In some cases, the target 21-34 age group was over-represented, and in others it was under-represented. Thus, the data lacked stability from quarter to quarter.

First Issue Recommendations:
- Incorporate a series of questions based on a more robust acculturation model in the questionnaire to determine the correct acculturation level of each respondent.
- The two primary data sources should be rerun and weighted in order to get a true picture of the state of the business. The weighting should be based on key demographic variables including age, gender, country of origin, and acculturation.
- Quotas should be established moving forward for country of origin, acculturation, gender, and age by market to ensure a more representative sample and to provide data stability across the quarterly measurement periods.

- The two legacy research suppliers should provide the client with a perspective on sample overall and by market based on the most recent U.S. Census Bureau figures every year so that the quotas are always based on these figures.
- The methodology should be standardized to ensure that both suppliers are using the same variables for the sake of consistency and in order to facilitate better integration across supplier data sets.

Second Issue: The Hispanic ending sample (the final number of respondents who completed the survey) was simply too small to be useful and wasn't in line with U.S. Census Bureau figures for each market (percent Hispanic of total population for each market).

- The sample wasn't robust enough to look at the data with confidence on a quarterly basis—it was only valid when looking at the larger, yearly aggregate.
- The ending sample would also not support breaking out the sample by acculturation level or any subgroup.
- The percentage of Hispanics by market wasn't in line with the U.S. Census Bureau figures— the research suppliers were using lower percentages, and thus undercounting Hispanic composition, across key Hispanic markets such as Chicago, Dallas, and Houston.

Second Issue Recommendations:
- Include Hispanic subsets in all total market tracking protocols. After all, it might be more efficient than creating a completely separate system to track Hispanic consumers.
- Increase the ending sample (proposed sample plan) so that it will provide the client with the ability to read a minimum of 100-plus consumers by acculturation group by quarter.

- The data needed to be weighted by acculturation level when reported out in total. The weighting should reflect predetermined weights by market as determined by data from Nielsen Spectra, or a similarly trustworthy source.

Third Issue: This issue involved which stores were being classified as Hispanic. The client was classifying stores based on the commonly used "percentage of patrons who are Hispanic" metric, but doing so in a way that caused evidentiary problems. The client was leaving control of this metric though to the frontline sales personnel, who often had incentives to be less than accurate. I found that it was a common practice for these sales people to change account classifications as a way of boosting Hispanic sales performance and thus the portion of their bonus that was tied to Hispanic sales.

Third Issue Recommendations:
- Update and validate Hispanic account classification and establish a consistent, recurring timeline for updating these classifications.
- Shift responsibility for Hispanic account classification away from sales personnel to avoid any potential for bias and conduct periodic, third party audits of these outlets instead.

The above examples serve as cautionary tales of an HPT system that lacked the requisite, underlying integrity and consequently harmed the company's Hispanic marketing efforts. This integrity is tremendously important to the Hispanic effort because as a potentially new and "prove it to me" effort at many companies that could be heavily scrutinized by skeptical senior management there is no room for error. Highly variable results from quarter to quarter and questionable underlying sources of data will not stand up to scrutiny. Nothing will more quickly damage the credibility of an HPT system, and damage the credibility of the Hispanic marketing effort more broadly, than dramatic swings in performance across adjacent measurement periods. Thus the need for analytical forensics—you have to get into the weeds.

Measurement Leads to Accountability

The above examples also illuminate the importance of identifying who will be responsible for Hispanic data quality control. In my experience, you have to be careful not to put a particular person or team in a position to be both judge and jury.

Keep in mind that any perceived tinkering with the underlying methodology might end up being fairly contentious. By this, I mean that you should expect some healthy debate and pushback from anyone whose performance is or will now be influenced by the HPT system. It is amazing to see how people that previously seemed somewhat disinterested in the Hispanic opportunity become especially engaged when they realize that their Hispanic performance will be quantitatively measured, and will then be widely reported within the organization. Herein lies one of the positive and often unintended consequences of establishing an HPT system: it is a highly effectively way to galvanize an organization and inject the Hispanic effort with more purpose and importance.

In order to succeed, the Hispanic business effort has to have teeth when it comes to broad and shared accountability, an idea I expand on in Chapter 10. Without an HPT system in place, it can be hard to pin down the issues that are holding the Hispanic effort back. Without accurate measurement you are relegating Hispanic marketing to its conventional status as an art versus a science, because as we all know, art is not something you measure or track. And with very little company-wide accountability, it becomes easy for people to make excuses. Measurement leads to transparency and clear accountability

The most important implication for the head of the Hispanic effort at Miller (which was me) was that all of a sudden it was a two-way street in terms of performance management. Prior to the establishment of the system, the accountability only seemed to flow in one direction; the Hispanic team was accountable to numerous constituents. The HPT system now empowered me as the head of the Hispanic effort and put me in a position to make the entire enterprise jointly accountable in terms of the Hispanic imperative. This was a transformative way to reposition the Hispanic team from being more of a reactive entity primarily focused on producing Spanish-language programming to the proactive champion of a more holistic, commercial effort.

Independent Store Audits

I want to briefly speak to a very helpful tool in the development of an HPT capability: independent store audits. Store audits can augment consumer insights and enable a company to measure Hispanic brand performance relative to competitors among consumers that can otherwise be difficult to access. In-store conditions can provide insight into drivers of performance from a retail perspective. Determining the store universe to audit typically consists of delineating stores that are in trading areas that are highly Hispanic and over index on harder to reach consumers, like unacculturated Hispanic consumers. This approach can be labor-intensive as it typically involves capturing retail sales by reviewing store receipts (given that many of these stores are cash-centric), which will provide client brand and competitive volume and share performance. During in-store visits, auditors can also capture retail drivers of performance such as the presence

of point of sale (POS) materials. An independent store audit read could deliver the following types of information:
- Share and volume performance
- Presence of POS by brand and by language
- Presence of and price of displays by brand

Given their labor-intensive nature, retail audits are typically expensive, but when it comes to the Hispanic market they can be worth their proverbial weight in gold as unmeasured outlets often play an outsized role in certain categories and in certain geographies.

8

HISPANIC RESEARCH PITFALLS

Over my 30-year career, I've managed or been involved with dozens of research projects that involve the Hispanic consumer, and I've been exposed to a number of systemic compromises that companies make that I want to address.

Compromise 1: Hispanic research is dominated by qualitative methodologies and often relies too heavily on in-person focus groups.

I don't think this dynamic serves our industry well, especially when Hispanic efforts are contrasted with those targeting the total market. Compared to a more rigorous, quantitative research report, a moderator's report from a series of Hispanic focus groups could seem overly simplistic and might reinforce the stereotype that the Hispanic effort lacks rigor.

There are a number of causes underlying this research inequality:
1. Hispanic marketing's overreliance on less expensive, qualitative methodologies is a direct outcome of more modest marketing research budgets. When less-than-rigorous results are produced, Hispanic marketing

efforts can then enter a pernicious cycle where they are not taken seriously by upper management and then suffer from chronic funding problems.
2. The overuse of focus groups in Hispanic research is a result of a focus on the less acculturated consumer, who are much more likely to engage in a focus group that might pay them a $100 incentive rather than participate in a lengthy and more intrusive survey administered by phone or the internet that might pay them a $10 incentive.
3. Many people I've encountered who are in charge of researching the Hispanic market are not classically trained market researchers. One my current clients moved into a Hispanic insights role after spending most of his career in brand activation. As you might have guessed, he is of Mexican descent. It is hardly surprising that he, as well others, tends to be more comfortable managing focus groups and is less inclined to lean into quantitative research given its inherent complexities.

Compromise 2: Recruiting unacculturated Hispanic consumers is challenging—so many companies make the mistake of not doing it.

I can't tell you how many challenging recruiting experiences I've encountered over the years whenever a research project involved unacculturated Hispanics. It's not that I'm surprised that this consumer segment is challenging to find and recruit; rather, I'm surprised that the research industry—and data collection companies, most specifically—have not made meaningful strides to improve their capabilities in this regard. In 2021, it is still challenging to find qualified respondents when one of the recruiting criteria is lower acculturation. For example, just as the COVID-19 pandemic was beginning, forcing governments to mandate lockdowns, I landed a research project from a major consumer packaged goods (CPG) client looking to launch a new brand that involved a series of eight online focus groups among Hispanics. The project required me to conduct two online focus groups each evening over the course of four nights, with each evening devoted to one of the four consumer segments that my client had identified in their Hispanic segmentation model.

One of these four segments was comprised of Hispanics who were less acculturated, lower-income, and Spanish-speaking dominant. I made a tragic mistake by letting my research fielding partner, a popular online focus group platform, schedule the two unacculturated Hispanic groups on the first night of fielding. Initial recruiting updates suggested that these first two groups were experiencing some expected recruiting challenges, but my research partner assured me that we would be fine come Monday. In a moment that now reminds me of the adage, "Insanity is doing the same thing over and over again and expecting different results," I went along with the plan, trusting that my recruiting partner would deliver as promised. After all, we were only hoping to connect with a total of 16 respondents that evening. At that point in time we were ignorant about how the pandemic was imposing disproportionate burdens on these lower-income, unacculturated Hispanics, so we naively wondered, how hard could it really be? To make matters worse, I had not considered that the product category we were studying was still significantly underdeveloped with this Hispanic segment, which made it especially difficult to find consumers who had ever tried any of the major brands in the category we were studying.

Suffice it to say that the first night of fielding turned out to be a complete disaster in terms of attendance. I'll spare you the details, but very few of the acculturated Hispanics we had recruited to participate were able to show up, my client was not happy, and I wondered if the entire project might be scrapped after such a disastrous first night. Late that evening, while still in a state of shock, I sprang into action and contacted Market-Ease, a firm that specializes in recruiting Hispanic consumers of all types, and which I had successfully used on many previous occasions. They came to the rescue and supplemented my research partner's underperforming recruiting process, which essentially saved the project and my relationship with the client in the end. I had made a big mistake: I was too concerned with managing costs, which I worried would soar too high if I utilized a third-party recruiting specialist, and was not concerned enough with the quality of the recruiting effort. I was being penny-wise and pound-foolish.

In the end, I internalized that nothing is more important than ensuring a quality recruit, especially when it comes to Hispanic efforts. Another important lesson is to always over-recruit these types of projects; hope for the best but assume the worst. While this anecdote involved qualitative research, I advocate approaching quantitative, survey-based research with the same level of caution.

Over the years, my firm has patched together hybrid recruiting solutions that were both tedious and necessary as part of large Hispanic segmentation projects for the likes of PepsiCo, AutoZone, and Anheuser-Busch. These projects intentionally used a more labor-intensive (and expensive) approach to data collection as all interviews had to be conducted in person, guided by a trained interviewer, and incorporated state-of-the-art computer-assisted personal interviewing (CAPI) software in order to minimize errors and make the user experience more engaging. My experience is that face-to-face interviews are essential for less-acculturated Hispanics given that this population often cannot read or write in English, might distrust phone interviews, and can be harder to access through the internet and by phone. It's for this reason that I get very nervous whenever a client tells me that it conducted research involving unacculturated Hispanic consumers exclusively over the internet. There's no doubt that internet penetration among unacculturated Hispanic consumers has improved dramatically over the years, especially given the capabilities of today's smartphones, but there's still no substitute for doing the hard work of face-to-face interviews.

Compromise 3: Hispanic research tends to cluster in a few familiar markets.

Ninety-nine percent of the Hispanic qualitative research projects I've been involved with have taken place in Los Angeles, Chicago, New York, Dallas, Houston, or Miami. Are there no qualified Hispanic respondents in other markets? If so, why is this the case? Not only do clients prefer to travel to these large metros, but most of the industry's focus group facilities are in these markets. But the quality of Hispanic research suffers whenever ease is prioritized over being representative.

A few years ago, a client called me to discuss a new Hispanic qualitative research project that had one unique string attached: it had to be conducted along the Texas-Mexico border. As I thanked him for the project, I did not let on that I was completely stumped by the geographic requirement given that, at that point, I had never ventured beyond the comfortable confines of the aforementioned major cities. As soon as I hung up the phone, I started scrambling to better understand what our options were. The client had stated a preference for El Paso, but my quick internet search revealed that there were no dependable focus group facilities on the U.S. side of the border, in part because the majority of this metro area (comprising over a million people) lived in nearby Juárez. There was one data collection company based in San Antonio (a seven and a half hour drive away) that advertised that they could conduct focus groups in El Paso. The only downside was that this approach involved setting up in a hotel room and using a closed-circuit camera connected to an adjacent room. This was a significant compromise, but I appreciated their "can do" mentality. I continued scouring for other options and eventually found a tiny, two-room, focus group facility in McAllen, Texas. Long story short, we ended up fielding several projects in this Rio Grande Valley town, and while the facility itself was a bit outdated and very small, the quality of the respondents' contributions was second to none. I learned my lesson: I had to get out of my comfort zone and go to where the consumer actually lived to get the insights I was looking for. After all, more than 90 percent of those living in the Rio Grande Valley are Hispanic.

Compromise 4: Proficient Spanish language moderators are hard to find.

I moderate a fair number of focus groups every year, the vast majority of which are conducted in English. I rarely moderate Spanish language groups given my Castilian accent and my rusty recall of many Spanish business terms, so I've consequently been exposed to many Spanish language moderators—and as much as it pains me to say this, most are really not that good. Why? In many cases, the bar has been set lower for them than for English-speaking moderators. They often get to hide behind the use of an interpreter, and thus are not scrutinized as much by English speaking clients. After all, the non-Spanish speaking client observing the groups behind a one-way mirror or remotely via streaming technology is actually not listening to the moderator, but is listening to the interpreter who translates what's being said in Spanish into English. These interpreters are invaluable to the process, but also inadvertently can mask a subpar moderator.

I used to work exclusively with one Spanish language moderator that always seemed to be booked, which created the impression that he must be really good, given he was always in such high demand. I was never particularly wowed by his moderating skills, but my clients seemed to like him a lot. On one project that we fielded in Austin, he had failed to show up to the focus group facility an hour in advance, which is when a moderator would typically arrive. He eventually arrived, but later, during a break in between groups, I asked him why he had cut things so close. As it turns out, his red eye flight from San Diego had run a little late, and he was running on only three hours of sleep. His subpar performance that night mirrored his punctuality, but guess what? The client in the back room was convinced he did an awesome job, in part because the interpreter made the moderator's questions seem fluid and coherent.

I'm also speaking from firsthand experience. I have to confess that on a recent focus group project I fielded in Phoenix I opted to also moderate the lone Spanish language group—the other two groups were conducted in English, for practical reasons. In all honesty, I was terrible, and if I had been on the other side of the one-way mirror, I would have fired me. I had the benefit of a very solid discussion guide, but I was very choppy in my communication with these respondents, as I failed to recall certain terms and struggled to track with the occasional Mexican slang. Make no mistake about it: I sucked. However, I had hired a terrific, local interpreter that more than made up for my foibles. I went back and visited with the client in the observation room during a scheduled break, and the client could not have been more thrilled or more oblivious. As I walked back to the focus group room, the interpreter looked up at me and winked. She clearly knew that she had bailed me out, and the familiarity of her wink seemed to suggest that this was not an isolated incident for her. I had learned my lesson (again): moderating Spanish language groups requires a strong Spanish-language moderator as well as a proven interpreter.

Compromise 5: Ethnicity and race are often treated interchangeably.

Across my work, I have often seen a research recruiting screener—the tool that marketers use to screen people into a research study based on how they identify themselves—label "Hispanic" as a race instead of as an ethnicity. For instance, the following question, which was recently passed along to me by a client, was included in a recruiting screener developed by another agency:

Example of a flawed approach:
- Which of the following best describes your ethnicity? (Select one answer)
    a. Caucasian/White
    b. African American
    c. Asian/Pacific Islander
    d. Hispanic/Latino
    e. Other: _____

Clearly only one of these, Hispanic, is an ethnicity while the others are races. While the nuances between these categories are more complex, in basic terms, race describes physical traits, while ethnicity alludes to cultural factors, like a similar place of origin or linguistic tradition. But why do these distinctions matter, especially for the purposes of marketing? In essence, this type of imprecise approach reinforces my earlier assertion that Hispanic marketing sometimes lacks precision and consistency. This in turn erodes the credibility of the entire effort we refer to as Hispanic marketing. As an industry, we have to stop cutting corners and accepting this type of shoddy work. Someone can identify as Hispanic, but not Latino, or someone can identify as belonging to more than one racial or ethnic group, and these differences in self-identification matter for efforts to market to certain groups. The questions asked in screeners should reflect these nuances.

Here's an example of a better approach to screening Hispanic consumers as part of a research study:

Example of an appropriate approach:
- Are you of Hispanic, Latino or Spanish origin? (Select one answer)
   a. Yes
   b. No

- What is your race? (Select all that apply)
   a. White
   b. Black or African American
   c. Asian
   d. American Indian or Alaska Native
   e. Native Hawaiian or Other Pacific Islander

These questions, which mirror the approach used by the U.S. Census Bureau, appropriately take both ethnicity and race into consideration when asking a respondent to self-identify. It also allows for respondents to choose more than one option where appropriate. Keep in mind that in the eyes of the Census Bureau (and mine), Hispanics can be of any race.

Compromise 6: Many acculturation models are overly simplistic.

Acculturation understandably plays a unique and outsized role in Hispanic marketing. The acculturation level of a specific consumer is typically determined through an acculturation model, which asks a respondent a series of questions. The responses to these questions are typically assigned a specific number of points, and the cumulative total of these points then determines whether the person is classified as unacculturated, bicultural, or acculturated. I've seen many versions of acculturation models, so I know that some are overly simplistic. While acculturation is a complicated concept that involves a number of factors, many of these models only take into consideration the degree to which Spanish or English is spoken in certain situations. Here's an example:

- How often do you personally speak Spanish and/or English in the following situations. For each situation, please indicate the language(s) you use:

RANDOMIZE LIST	Only English	English More Than Spanish	Spanish & English Equally	Spanish More Than English	Only Spanish
With your parents or older family members	1	2	3	4	5
With your friends or neighbors	1	2	3	4	5
With your coworkers or acquaintances	1	2	3	4	5
When you listen to the radio	1	2	3	4	5
When you watch TV	1	2	3	4	5

POINTS:	ASSIGNMENT:
Only English = 1 Point	5 – 10 Points = Acculturated
English More Than Spanish = 2 Points	
Spanish & English Equally = 3 Points	11 – 19 Points = Bicultural
Spanish More Than English = 4 Points	20 – 25 Points = Unacculturated
Only Spanish = 5 Points	

Each answer above is assigned a point total. Acculturation level is then assigned based on total points assigned.

A more robust approach should incorporate generational distance (e.g., the closer they are to their immigration roots), time spent in the U.S., a cultural identity profile of their friends, and more.

I should also note that the role of acculturation should never be to segment consumers for market strategy purposes. Acculturation should be used for media planning purposes once a brand's target consumer has been defined. That's because the key to segmentation is to identify discrete groups that are reachable, persuadable, and sizeable, and grouping people solely based on acculturation only tells you how big the groups are; it doesn't indicate how to actually reach or persuade the people in these groups, whose consumer habits likely vary widely. The reason acculturation should not be used for segmenting is that it only represents a few variables (and mostly demographic) of many to consider, and therefore normally it is not that predictive of consumer behavior.

I have seen companies successfully use attitudinally-based segmentation (correlated with category behavior) and occasion-based segmentation to segment Hispanic consumers. These companies would then overlay acculturation and other demographic variables to better understand the consumer (in an effort to identify and reach them for communication purposes). For example, as part of a segmentation study for a non-alcoholic beverage client, my firm identified a significant) segment that we called "habitual indulgers." If you looked at acculturation within this habitual indulger segment, you would see that there were acculturated, bicultural, and unacculturated individuals. Therefore, acculturation is not the main variable driving different usage rates of the beverage. There are certainly some categories where acculturation may explain category behavior (e.g., remittances), but these cases are in the minority. This is not to say that developing a better understanding of people based on acculturation is a fruitless endeavor; rather, I am saying that understanding their attitudes typically allows you to market to them effectively.

9

WITH WHOSE ARMY?

A former boss of mine used to like to ask "With whose army?" as a way of helping us understand that the best conceived strategies still require the right leadership and the right organization in order to succeed. I've spent the better part of the last two decades as a consultant, which has largely enabled me to make recommendations to clients and then leave it up to them how to actualize my plans. Obviously, it is a lot easier to give advice than it is to actually implement that advice. This chapter focuses on how to bring THM to life through the right leadership and the right organization. It isn't just about getting the right people with the right skillsets in place. It is also critical that the Hispanic business accountability be a "shared accountability" across the enterprise, which I will explore further in Chapter 10.

Structure Follows Strategy

Structure should always follow strategy. Once you have the Hispanic strategy in place, you will need a supporting organizational strategy and a plan for bringing it to life. By this, I mean a detailed plan that outlines the specific organizational structure and processes that need to be deployed. This includes people and competencies, roles and responsibilities, systems of accountability, management routines, decision rights, at both the headquarters and market levels. There are a number of ways to structure the Hispanic marketing team that depend primarily on 1) the importance of the Hispanic market to the company, and 2) to what extent a company intends to embed the sub-function within the broader marketing organization (i.e., integrated versus isolated):

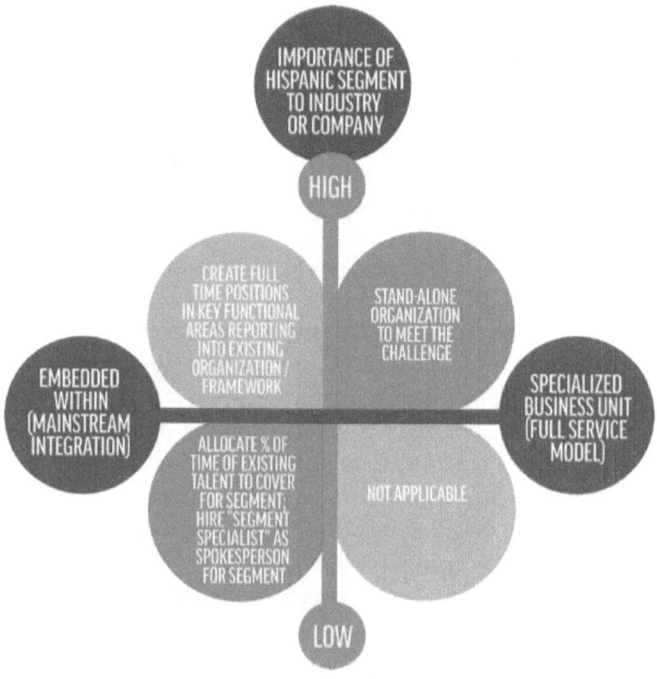

Figure 9: Importance of Segment to Industry or Company

Other key considerations when building or reorganizing a Hispanic Marketing team include:
- What capabilities are needed to deliver the plan?

- What should this team actually do itself versus what should it outsource?
- How should the roles be differentiated/delineated between headquarters and local markets? How does this inform the requisite competencies of each?
- How should you manage the complexities inherent to having multiple personnel involved with the Hispanic business? What specific tools, processes, and systems are needed?

Does It Take a Hispanic?

Not every organization will have a large team dedicated to the Hispanic market opportunity, but many will have at least one person leading the charge. This leads me to an age-old question: Does it take a Hispanic to market to Hispanics? The results of a survey my firm fielded years ago in conjunction with the executive search firm Heidrick & Struggles revealed that heads of marketing were essentially split on whether it is really necessary for those marketing to Hispanics to be Hispanic themselves. I've always felt that the more important qualifications are a strong strategic marketing acumen and an ability to think out of the box. Don't get me wrong: I do fundamentally believe that being Hispanic can certainly help you be a more effective Hispanic advertising creative, but it should not be an essential criterion for the development of Hispanic marketing strategy. One of my clients appointed a non-Hispanic person to head up their Hispanic efforts, and it didn't take long before other (Hispanic) people at the company complained that the decision was flawed because this appointee was not Hispanic. I knew this individual well and had no doubt that he would be an incredibly effective marketer to Hispanics because he is both an accomplished strategic marketer and inquisitive. Let's face it, we have all met people heading up Hispanic marketing teams that seem to be just going through the motions. Who would you rather have focused on the Hispanic opportunity at your company?

Contributory Negligence

Here's another example that helps prove my case: I once asked a middle manager of Hispanic descent on the Hispanic marketing team of one of my clients why he thought he was uniquely qualified to dispense marketing advice about Hispanics to an organization that was mostly comprised of non-Hispanics. He responded: "Well, since I am Hispanic, I can relate better to the target (than non-Hispanics) and that makes me an expert on this group." I found this to be a rather cavalier answer and realized that Hispanic marketers themselves were guilty of perpetuating this myth—another example of contributory negligence. I wanted to probe a bit further to make sure I was not missing some other nuanced rationale, so I asked, "What is the source of your Hispanic expertise beyond simply being Hispanic?"

His response troubled me even more: "In my previous role, I marketed tortillas to Hispanics and so I understand what it takes to market to them. This category is no different." Keep in mind that the category in question was alcoholic beverages. Imagine my surprise when I was supposed to believe that marketing tortillas primarily to Hispanic moms was somehow analogous to selling alcoholic beverages to Hispanic young adults. I was floored. This self-appointed Hispanic expert did not understand that Hispanic marketing was no different than marketing to any consumer group; it is fundamentally all about segmentation, targeting, and positioning. It's not about whether you know who J Balvin or Bad Bunny are; it's more about whether you understand how to develop a winning targeting strategy for a complex and heterogeneous group of consumers.

Stop Waving the Flag

This sets up one of my fundamental beliefs that intentionally challenges the way many Hispanic marketers, consultants, and agencies do business. A few years ago, I was visiting with Rob Lynch—back when he was an executive at Heinz; he's now the CEO of Papa John's—to kick off a new engagement where we also discussed Heinz's search for a head of Hispanic marketing. One of the key points I reinforced was the need to hire for a specific skillset versus a specific demographic profile. At the end of the meeting, Rob noted how relieved he was by my feedback. "I thought you were going to advocate that the new hire had to be Hispanic," he revealed.

I went on to explain to him that my advocacy is first and foremost for the client and for the opportunity that the Hispanic market represents. I don't confuse this with advocacy for all things Hispanic, which I do feel strongly about in my personal life. This is where many folks in this industry get off track. This is business—it's not politics, and it's not community relations. Too many marketers in this space lose sight of this very simple truth: marketing to Hispanics is about commerce and it is not about "waving the flag." Let's not confuse this with Simon Sinek's *Start With Why* book and movement to have companies declare and live their values, which is a completely different topic. Don't get me wrong: I have some fundamentally strong beliefs about the role and importance of the Hispanic community in the U.S. along with some real concerns about equality, and I am free to pursue those issues in my personal life through the support of certain advocacy groups and by using the power of the ballot.

Talent Trumps Ethnicity

Now back to the main focus of this chapter: who should lead the team focused on the Hispanic opportunity? I'm going to take it a step further; not only do I not think that it takes a Hispanic to market to Hispanics, but I actually believe that in many cases the best thing an organization can do is put a high performing non-Hispanic in the role for several reasons:

1. It communicates to the organization that winning with Hispanic consumers is a strategic priority that will require the best and the brightest regardless of their ethnicity. In some ways, this is similar to what Procter & Gamble did years ago in terms of its vaunted Walmart team. Understandably, very few of the high performers at P&G's Cincinnati headquarters wanted to relocate to a town in Northwest Arkansas—one of the poultry processing capitals of the world. Not only were there quality of life concerns, but there was a fear of getting stranded out there with no lifeline back to headquarters. Eventually P&G's leadership changed perceptions of the Walmart team by making it a desirable, high-profile assignment that only leads to bigger and better career opportunities. P&G's upper management made it clear that Walmart experience would be a career accelerant. This repositioning of the team and its roles created one of the most successful talent migrations in recent history. P&G now has a long track record of placing company stars in the lead Walmart role. Ironically, and partly as a result of P&G's visionary move, *U.S. News & World Report* rated the Fayetteville-Springdale-Rogers Metropolitan Statistical Area in 2019 as the fourth best place to live in the U.S.

2. Hiring a non-Hispanic high performer also communicates overtly to the organization that Hispanic marketing is not a dead-end career path and that it will not pigeonhole you. This is a very real concern for many marketers of Hispanic descent and is why many of them steer clear from Hispanic marketing roles.

3. It provides future leaders of the organization with an important and formative multicultural experience that will help them dispel myths and challenge paradigms when they eventually ascend to senior leadership roles in the future.
4. It injects new thinking and energy into roles that have, in many cases, been saddled with incumbents of Hispanic descent who have lost that fire in the belly.
5. It can also help address the inadvertent ostracism that sometimes creeps into organizations (e.g., "I don't need to worry about it since I'm sure the Hispanic team is covering that."). One of the biggest obstacles Hispanic marketing teams face in terms of reaching their full potential involves integrating with the total market team's efforts. Hiring a non-Hispanic to the Hispanic team helps encourage the broader marketing organization to see the Hispanic opportunity as part of the overall effort rather than a distinct and separate effort. I've actually observed situations where a total market brand team actually thinks of the Hispanic marketing team as a quasi-competitor in a contest for mutually exclusive resources.

As I mentioned in Chapter 2, examining how multinationals go to market in foreign markets also provides an important analog to the previous topic on how to staff a Hispanic marketing team. Why is it that Procter & Gamble can send a Japanese high-performer to Chile or Unilever can send one of its marketing hot shots from the UK to Mexico? Another great example is Anheuser-Busch, given that here in the U.S. almost their entire senior leadership team is Brazilian. Why is it that these companies don't always staff key roles with local personnel? Because they have learned through trial and error that skillset and experience always trump nationality or country of origin. I wholeheartedly believe this same principle should apply to Hispanic marketing in the U.S.

As I discuss in Chapter 5, I am a believer that Hispanic cultural nuances should influence the development of creative, but not the development of marketing strategy. Thus, I propose that you look to your Hispanic agencies for deep cultural understanding and ensure that the folks you place in charge of Hispanic marketing are fundamentally sound, strategic marketers above all else. If you are still tempted to staff these roles with Hispanics, I strongly encourage you to do so with marketers who have had at least one significant experience in the organization's total market team, and ideally on the key brand in question, so that they understand the big picture and how Hispanic marketing fits into the larger objectives of the company.

Hispanic Siberia

Unfortunately, our industry has created a vicious circle when it comes to staffing Hispanic marketing roles: by defaulting to a person with a Hispanic surname, many companies inadvertently have created what I refer to as "Hispanic Siberia." This is that place where no promising marketer of Hispanic descent ever wants to end up: the place where someone is stereotyped into being a Hispanic marketer and is assumed not capable of much more. What then ends up happening is quite insidious:

- Marketers of Hispanic descent land in Hispanic Siberia and can never get out, which creates a team full of Hispanic old timers with gold 25th anniversary watches. This structure becomes an impediment to any new talent joining their ranks because the old timers aren't going anywhere, so there is rarely an opportunity for someone new to take on an important role. This in turn keeps the Hispanic marketing function stale and outdated, and it tends to fall further and further behind the sophistication of the total market efforts.

- At the same time, high performers look over at what is going on in Hispanic Siberia and do everything in their power to stay clear of its borders. This in turn continues to reinforce the perception that Hispanic marketing is a marginally important function since it is so hard to recruit talent.

So, what do I recommend to avoid these problems? A very straightforward three-pronged approach to staffing Hispanic marketing leadership roles:

1. Be agnostic about ethnicity: Only appoint high performers and ignore what their last name or ancestry is. After all, it makes sense to put your best people in the positions that align with the best growth opportunities. The Hispanic marketing function can and should be an important developmental opportunity and rotational assignment.
2. Make it commensurately senior: Ensure that the leader of this Hispanic marketing capability is at the same level as the other roles that report directly into the CMO; if most are director level roles, then make the Hispanic role a director level role, and if most of the CMO's direct reports are vice presidents, then ensure that the Hispanic leadership role is commensurate. Inconsistency here communicates a lot. Most importantly, make sure that the head of this capability reports directly to the CMO and not to some level in between. In cases where the Hispanic business team is truly cross-functional, it might even be preferable to have the role report directly to the chief executive, as was the case when the Vice President of Multicultural Development reported directly to Michael Eisner at Disney. I've seen many companies that have a junior person in the lead Hispanic role who does not report directly to the CMO. Once again, this is where I see a lack of discipline; if the head of your marketing efforts is not senior enough to report to the CMO, then find

someone who is, rather than minimizing the entire effort. There is one additional, pragmatic reason to ensure that the head of the Hispanic effort reports to a member of the C-suite: if they don't have a seat at the table when budgets are being fought over, who will advocate for the Hispanic opportunity? Herein lies one of the most important responsibilities of this leadership role: to advocate for the Hispanic opportunity through a well-constructed business case.
3. Create explicit exit strategies: Ensure that tenures within the Hispanic Marketing team are of a fixed and predictable duration no longer than three years; people in these roles need to rotate in and then rotate out. Furthermore, and assuming that performance warrants it, ensure that successful leaders of the Hispanic effort are rewarded with a subsequent promotion outside of the Hispanic team. A stint on the Hispanic marketing team should convey to other employees that the Hispanic team is a career accelerant rather than a professional dead end.

Cultural Sensibility

I wanted to spend some time debunking another Hispanic staffing myth: the so-called need for candidates to have "cultural sensibility." During a meeting with a client who heads up the Hispanic effort for one of the largest consumer products companies in the country and whose business disproportionately relies on Hispanic consumers, we discussed the requirements for success when staffing Hispanic leadership roles. While we agreed on many of the aforementioned points in this chapter, we hit a bit of an impasse when he declared:

"The leader of Hispanic marketing does need to be strategic and not simply have a Hispanic surname, but they need to be able to understand cultural nuances.... They have to have the right cultural sensibility; they can't just be someone who looks at numbers and makes decisions based on data. They have to have a gut feel."

I was shocked to see someone I otherwise agreed with say something so untethered to the real material needs of a company. Our industry has propagated this myth for so long that so many of us repeat it without really thinking it through. I do agree that a cultural sensibility can be helpful, but a focus solely on culture often becomes a distracting element. Let me explain through a real world example. Another one of my firm's clients has unfortunately embraced this fallacy to the point that they are not focusing their efforts on strategy, but instead are focusing on actually doing the ad agency's job. They are not focused on segmentation, targeting, and positioning or on engagement models, but instead they are focused on which up and coming Latin music group they should sign and create a marketing platform with. In my opinion, this is clearly a task that should be assigned to an agency since they should, in theory, be much better attuned to cultural trends than the client. We often see this dynamic at play when agency people move over to the client side, and when they realize they are not yet comfortable with marketing strategy, they gravitate back to the familiar: selling culture and "big ideas." This is yet another area where Hispanic marketing industry has developed some bad habits. Why is it so common for Hispanic agency personnel to jump into client Hispanic marketing roles? This is not as common on the total market side of the enterprise. This has inadvertently lowered the bar on what it takes to be a great marketer to Hispanics by reinforcing that it is all about culture and advertising. I am not sure if it is intentional or not, but it continues to feed the Univision and Telemundo Spanish language commercial machine. Everything seems to point to an industry that has gorged on self-interest and as a result has not kept pace with its peer effort on the total market side.

Despite these cautions, I do totally agree that hiring

someone with a nuanced understanding of the culture and even the language can be helpful in terms of keeping the agency in check. I want to refer to one such case. You might recall from earlier chapters that Miller Brewing had previously hired Randy Ransom, who was a very seasoned marketer from Coke to head up its Hispanic efforts. The brewery had finally turned the corner and handed the keys to someone with the right skillset, mentality, and gravitas to get the job done. While this former Coke marketer was originally from Mexico City, he more importantly had one of the strongest marketing pedigrees imaginable after serving as the CMO for FEMSA Cerveza, Mexico's second largest brewer at the time, and then serving as the SVP of the Coca-Cola trademark business in the U.S. Not to mention a previous stint in Southeast Asia working for the best in class global marketing team at The Coca-Cola Company. Plus, earlier in his career he had spent time at the firm then known as Casanova-Pendrill, one of the first really successful Hispanic ad agencies. So, in theory this guy had it all and in many ways was grossly overqualified for the lead Hispanic marketing role at the brewery. Whereas most companies tend to under-hire for their Hispanic leadership role, the brewery intentionally did quite the opposite and hired a true heavy hitter to lead the effort. However, it is important and somewhat disappointing to note that despite hiring someone with amazing talent and experience, the brewery has never fully capitalized on the Hispanic opportunity, which highlights that the Hispanic effort requires a lot more than a talented leader with a clear vision.

Enablers and Alliances

THM also requires some key organizational enablers and alliances for it to take root and succeed. No enabler is more important than an engaged and supportive CMO who champions the Hispanic team within the organization.

A supportive CMO is critical if Hispanic marketers are going to gain any access to the executive team and if they ever hope to secure the Hispanic effort a place on the CEO's leadership agenda. When I spoke to a former colleague of mine who was heading up the Hispanic effort at a large CPG company, I asked him how things were going since he was new to the Hispanic space and had moved over from a more traditional, total market, brand management role. His answer both surprised and disappointed me: "I've loved the autonomy. No one gets in the way, and frankly, I don't think my boss really cares too much about the Hispanic team at all." Even though Hispanics alone accounted for around two-thirds of this particular category's expected growth over the next decade, the CMO didn't really care!

A pervasive problem that is challenging to overcome is how to convert a reluctant CMO into a believer. This is difficult to accomplish given the myriad of other priorities that most CMOs face. Here too is where I think THM can come in handy: in practice, it essentially means applying more discipline and mirroring the rigor and processes we often see in other parts of the business. For example, it will behoove you to develop a tight alliance with the folks in your corporate strategy group (if your organization has one). Those same people that are tasked with identifying long-term growth opportunities can be your allies and an important constituency. Unfortunately, most companies silo the Hispanic effort away from the corporate strategy effort given the highly sensitive nature of the latter group's work, but the two should converge to some extent. This group typically has the CEO's ear and oftentimes reports directly into the CEO, which can be a tremendous advantage if you are trying to get their attention. Lastly, it is important to note that this potential ally has two things the Hispanic team typically does not have: credibility with senior management as well as superior analytical capabilities and resources (e.g., key data, vendors, access to proven consultants, etc.). It can be a marriage made in heaven.

Another group that you should build a bridge to is the community affairs team (again, assuming your organization has one). Too often the community affairs effort is also decoupled from the larger Hispanic strategy and effort, which can result in inefficiencies and even conflict. Most of the time this group is focused on external Hispanic constituencies like the U.S. Hispanic Chamber of Commerce or other trade associations. This team has a very different mission than the commercial mission of the Hispanic business team, but ensuring that both sides are talking to each other and looking for synergies is especially important. However, it is also important that the head of Hispanic not be diverted into these activities too often (e.g., speaking engagements, conferences, etc.), as that should be the purview of the community affairs team or even the CEO. I am highly skeptical of companies who take their Hispanic business lead and also assign them community outreach responsibilities as they are inadvertently setting up these individuals for failure; you simply can't be a goodwill ambassador and an effective marketer at the same time. A simple rule of thumb is that the head of the Hispanic marketing effort should be focused on the consumer, while the head of the Hispanic community affairs effort should be focused on all the other external constituencies.

Supporting Entities

The last topic I want to briefly speak to in this chapter is the importance of establishing entities that provide other types of support, such as governance and insights: namely a Hispanic Steering Committee and a Hispanic User Panel. I describe them both below on an illustrative basis.

Hispanic Steering Committee:
Description: A senior, advisory group comprised of sales and marketing personnel that act as a functional Board of Directors for the head of the Hispanic effort. This bilateral group can create value by:
- Driving alignment and coordination between marketing and sales in terms of Hispanic business plan.
  - Monitoring progress vs. Hispanic KPIs.
  - Monitoring obstacles to success and course correcting as necessary.
- Facilitating clear and consistent understanding of the Hispanic strategy and imperatives.
  - Reinforcing the purpose of upcoming programs.
- Creating bilateral accountability in the quest to fully harvest Hispanic consumers' business potential.
- Providing a forum for timely direction and decisions on commercial issues affecting the Hispanic business.
  - Providing approvals: strategy, project charters, and resource allocation.
- Tracking and ensuring progress of mission-critical Hispanic projects.
- Providing leadership, consultation, and teaching to the organization in terms of the Hispanic opportunity.
- Providing a forum for the exchange of best practices which are scalable to other geographies.

Hispanic User Panel:
Description: An advisory panel made up of company personnel that are the true "on the street" Hispanic champions from across the country. The panel's purpose is to provide a feedback loop mechanism from the front lines back to the Hispanic marketing team at headquarters. They are your reality check.

10

SHARED ACCOUNTABILITY

In order to succeed on a sustained basis, the Hispanic effort at most companies requires that accountability extend beyond the Hispanic marketing team. Sustained success requires broader accountability across the organization, both in terms of breadth and depth. By breadth I mean that the accountability has to extend beyond the marketing function to other functions like sales. By depth I mean that the accountability needs to extend up into the ranks of senior management.

Depth of Accountability

First and foremost, the Hispanic initiative must be endorsed at the highest levels of an organization; it will not reach its full potential if the explicit endorsement and active engagement of senior management aren't in place. By the way, one without the other is not enough: success requires both. As noted earlier, I have experienced firsthand the power of this THM guiding principle, but endorsement and active engagement must also be accompanied by clear and visible accountability. It was only after Miller Brewing's executive committee added the

Hispanic business to its key performance indicators and labeled the effort a "mission critical project" did the rest of the organization really begin to think of the Hispanic opportunity as an imperative rather than simply an opportunity. Keep in mind that referring to the Hispanic market as just an "opportunity" implies that Hispanic marketing efforts can be optional or just a "nice to have." At the brewery, the Hispanic effort now had gravitas. The brewery had seemingly put all the right pieces in place starting with an over-qualified leader of the Hispanic team (who later became CMO), a best in class team, as well as an industry-leading financial commitment.

But despite all of these very visible and compelling building blocks, there was still tacit resistance across some parts of the enterprise in terms of the true priority that the Hispanic business represented. After all, the system had heard all the promising talking points before followed by the fits and starts that have come to typify so many Hispanic efforts. Having the chief executive or the entire executive team explicitly sign up for a Hispanic objective is tantamount to letting the genie out of the bottle—nothing is more transformative. However, engagement from senior leadership is not a silver bullet. Executive team accountability is really an "outcome variable" that results after a lot of other capability building and hard work is in place. There isn't an executive team in America that is going to sign up for a Hispanic imperative that directly impacts their compensation without a lot of prior due diligence and without first putting the organization in a position to win. Senior management objectives typically cause spasms within an organization. At first, the enterprise will only give the Hispanic effort lip service as the executive team's support structure prepares its quarterly stewardship reports—when it is fleetingly top of mind—but with time, it will become ingrained. Of course, this key enabler is always at the mercy of a change in leadership, and thus the inherent vulnerability of this effort always hovers threateningly. The most effective way to insulate the Hispanic marketing effort from the whims of each new senior administration is to enact the principles of Transformational Hispanic Marketing, and thereby reinforce both the validity and rigor of the Hispanic marketing discipline.

Breadth of Accountability

Senior leadership accountability must also be accompanied by broader enterprise accountability, especially the sales function. This accountability breadth coincides with the aforementioned evolution from seeing the Hispanic opportunity as merely a marketing effort, to thinking and operating as a more holistic, Hispanic business. In organizations where Hispanic efforts are still the exclusive domain of the marketing folks, accountability has been siloed and typically has not extended beyond the Hispanic team, and thus not everyone needs to buy in. Under this all too common scenario, the Hispanic effort will continue to be a non-starter. New behaviors, attitudes, and beliefs can only be institutionalized through shared accountability—and through both depth and breadth of accountability. In many cases, Hispanic consumers are an afterthought, and the organization isn't giving the Hispanic opportunity all the attention it warrants.

Sometimes It Requires a Mandate

Sometimes, drastic steps need to be taken in order to jar some sense into an organization and break some long-standing norms; sometimes, it is necessary for senior management to also declare a mandate regarding the Hispanic business. This is similar to the leadership principles that Amazon has used to build its culture or Ray Dalio's book *Principles for Success*. Here's a solid example of a senior management mandate relating to the Hispanic business: All brand and functional groups must recognize and consider how to capitalize on the Hispanic consumer growth opportunity across all relevant strategic and operational initiatives.

This shared accountability has to occur not just at the corporate level but also at the brand, geographic unit, distributor or wholesaler, and retailer levels. The Hispanic imperative needs to be relevant to middle management and, where applicable, also relevant to frontline employees. It is important to define for the organization what it will take to win across the value chain.

11

THE HISPANIC SOCIALIZATION PLAN

How do you enable and accelerate adoption of the Hispanic strategy across the organization? After all, different parts of the organization are likely to be in different stages of the Hispanic adoption journey.

You can't just assume that a sound Hispanic business strategy and plan will magically permeate throughout the organization. The Hispanic business strategy must be supported by an intentional and ongoing socialization plan. Whoever takes on leadership of this socialization effort needs to think of themselves as being on the vanguard and take on the mindset of an evangelist.

A number of years ago, my firm was hired by PepsiCo to help develop a segmentation of the U.S. Hispanic consumer. The project was exhaustive and took a long time to execute given the client's various divisions and constituencies. Shortly after my firm finished the last deliverable of the engagement, I was introduced to the brand team that ran the company's second largest brand franchise: Mountain Dew. This was a very successful franchise, with considerable momentum, but one that had historically underperformed with Hispanics. Given how well the Hispanic segmentation had been received, I was then invited to be part of this Mountain Dew team's extensive innovation effort and was given a seat at the table as the Hispanic strategy agency. I took part in various workshops and offsites and quickly realized that this brand team, despite its best intentions, did not have a fundamentally sound understanding of the Hispanic opportunity and was unfamiliar with the outcomes of the segmentation work we had developed a couple of months earlier.

During these meetings I was reminded of how hard it is for brand teams to keep the Hispanic opportunity top of mind given all the other priorities they typically have to manage. This struggle managing competing priorities is not a unique situation, as in my experience, institutional memory tends to be short when it comes to the Hispanic effort. This in turn makes the evangelist role of the Hispanic marketing team increasingly difficult and creates the need for a very deliberate socialization effort. This type of socialization requires a stewardship framework that establishes internal targets (key constituents), a set of tools, and communication cadences to help drive ongoing awareness and understanding of the Hispanic growth opportunity. Structured socialization is particularly important when the preceding work reveals findings that challenge longstanding organizational paradigms. The socialization effort needs to be planned ahead of time and executed methodically rather than on an ad hoc basis. In many dynamic consumer-packaged goods companies, this is particularly important given the revolving door of talent that results from the constant rotational assignments and rapid promotions.

Poor institutional memory and record keeping is not intentional; it is an unintended, though unfortunate, consequence. As a result, Hispanic socialization efforts tend to be reactive, episodic, and too reliant on inefficient, one-on-one advocacy. It is essentially impossible for one person to maintain the required level of advocacy, evangelism, and socialization in medium to large organizations. In all but the smallest organizations, these efforts simply can't be executed on a one-on-one basis, especially given all the competing priorities and responsibilities that middle managers have. This predicament in turn allows key constituencies to either ignore or unintentionally forget the Hispanic opportunity, resulting in very low share of mind on an ongoing basis (and thus the constant need for reinforcement). What is needed is an efficient and actively managed effort that creates familiarity at scale and generates broader impact. In other words, it requires amplification.

Best Practices

As part of the aforementioned innovation engagement for Mountain Dew, my firm was charged with identifying best practices across other industries and thus reached out to the Head of the Hispanic Marketing at one of the largest mobile phone companies in the country, T-Mobile. We talked in detail about how he managed the Hispanic socialization effort, an often overlooked and critically important dimension to building a successful enterprise-wide understanding of the Hispanic opportunity. This very experienced Hispanic marketing expert explained how he personally delivered a Hispanic business overview to every single new employee that joined their extended marketing organization (among other socialization activities in his toolbox). Building a custom, Hispanic socialization plan is going to depend on each organization's specific context, needs, and capabilities. That said, THM suggests that any Hispanic socialization effort:

- Have a champion within senior management (not just the person heading up the Hispanic effort)

- Be thought of and built to be continuous and not episodic or ad hoc (meaning that the organization must be continuously engaged)
- Specify:
  - Who are your key constituents?
  - What is the call plan for each?
  - What do we need to communicate?
  - With what frequency?
  - Through which mechanisms?

At this stage you are probably asking yourself, "With whose army?" I realize this and other aspects of THM can sound a little dreamy, and that you will have to take into account the practical limitations of your context and its capacity constraints. That said, the premise behind this ongoing socialization imperative is that in the long run you will save time, and your overall Hispanic efforts will tend to experience less regression.

I have found that workshops are an effective embedding technique that can create scale for the Hispanic socialization effort and generate several key benefits. They:
1. Help assimilate key information and get all key stakeholders on the same page.
2. Encourage stakeholder ownership and commitment to implementation.
3. Facilitate the development of action plans by functional area or group.

The other socialization tool that can be very helpful is a video that helps bring the Hispanic strategy and target consumer to life. If you have the benefit of agency support, they can be a tremendous asset in helping you create these types of socialization tools that provide scale and efficiency.

The other thing that you are probably thinking at this point is that all of this socialization work requires financial resources. Yes, it does. That is why you have to budget for it. When I worked at Coke, we spent a lot of money on sponsorships. The company also had a rule of thumb that you could not sign a new sponsorship without also budgeting for its activation (e.g., setting aside funds to create a sweepstakes promotion that involved winning tickets to the team's games or setting aside funds to build out in stadium branding that connected your brand to the team in question). After all, what good is signing a deal with the Milwaukee Brewers but then not having any budget left over to activate that marketing asset? The same principle applies here: you must budget for Hispanic socialization or it won't happen.

AFTERWORD

Over the years many articles, books, and new business pitches have been written about the promising Hispanic market opportunity and how to market to Hispanics. There are also dozens of agencies that claim to specialize in the Hispanic market. It is estimated that advertisers spend upward of $9 billion a year targeting this demographic. Yet one can make the case that the field of Hispanic marketing has not evolved much over the past couple of decades. To put it bluntly, this industry is stuck in a rut. MediaPost indicates that Hispanic ad dollars only represent 6 percent of the total U.S. ad spend, yet Hispanics comprise over 19 percent of the total population.[9] There have been many explanations for this significant underspend, but I would argue that one of the most insidious reasons is that Hispanic marketing as an

---

[9] Karla Fernandez Parker, "Why Advertisers Are Underspending On Hispanic Market," MediaPost, December 16, 2019, https://www.mediapost.com/publications/article/344630/why-advertisers-are-underspending-on-hispanic-mark.html.

industry has not made a consistent and compelling business case for these funds.

Significant aspects of Hispanic marketing are fundamentally broken and antiquated. Transformational Hispanic Marketing challenges conventional wisdom, makes the case that the field of Hispanic marketing needs to be transformed, and that it's time for the industry to raise its standards. This book focuses on how to build the foundational and strategic capabilities that will help modernize this discipline.

This book also highlights how many companies routinely accept a number of significant compromises that impede building a successful and enduring Hispanic marketing capability. One of the factors that holds the industry back is a lack of strategic rigor and consistency. Thus, this book is not just about helping companies propel their Hispanic marketing efforts forward, it is also about helping companies avoid regression. Transformational Hispanic Marketing is designed to change behavior on an enduring basis and to provide Hispanic marketing efforts with a more reliable foundation.

APPENDIX

Material in support of Chapter 7: Hispanic Performance Tracking

Getting an effective HPT system and up and running requires not only time, and resources, but a well thought out approach. I have found that it is helpful to start the process with the development of a project charter. Here's an illustrative HPT System Project Charter:

The Task at Hand

To agree on and develop a holistic and integrated HPT System that includes business measures (e.g., volume), brand equity measures, and other salient information (e.g., media investment) so as to understand how [Company or brand name] strategy and initiatives are impacting its business and marketing objectives overall and by key market. This system will represent a significant capability enhancement to the overall Hispanic business imperative and is instrumental in the Hispanic team's evolution to greater thought leadership and the development of a framework for success. Most importantly the implementation of this tool will enable us to make the Hispanic imperative a true KPI for the company.

Success Factors (What Success Will Look Like)
- Ensure you are tracking the KPI's that drive the business and link back to the business case
- Must take into account HQ needs as well as the needs of the local markets (we often find that the Hispanic tracking system doesn't take the needs of the local market into account).
- What is the level of analysis, synthesis and recommendation we will provide to constituents? It is imperative that the due diligence be conducted to ensure that the system will actually be used.
- Initially focus on one brand. The solution must be scalable in order to include additional brands in the future.
- The data driving the metrics must ideally come from one single source.
- We can't just serve up a data dump and have to create a true Hispanic business dashboard; one where information actually leads to insights.
- KPIs must be measured with confidence (minimize data variance).
- Metrics must be reported for total Hispanics and acculturation groups and compared to non-Hispanics.
- For the volume tracking, class of trade specific and chain specific metrics are needed.
- The system must be up and running in time to impact calendar [Year].

Charting the Course (How Are We Going to Get It Done?)
- Develop a cross functional steering committee consisting of senior management in order to gain

alignment and gain commitment from the entire organization.
- Develop a stakeholder management plan (who, what, and how often).
- Dividing and conquering based on ownable pieces of work (given the desire to have a system up and running to impact fiscal year 2021).
  - Develop working team and extended teams based on competencies to get it done.
- Provide a clear and consistent understanding of the project and the objectives by:
  - Defining the work streams.
  - Defining the overall objectives and by work stream.
  - Defining the working team for each work stream with clear roles, responsibilities, and timing.
- Tracking performance against project objectives and timing consistently.
- Holding team members accountable.

The Work Streams
- <u>Work Stream #1</u>: Volume Tracker—Volume and other key business measures to track for the Hispanic market
  - To develop a volume tracking system for Hispanic segment by agreeing on and defining key performance indicators for client at the HQ and local market level.
  - Data to be stratified by Hispanic market, acculturation level, class of trade, key chains, and compared to non-Hispanic.
  - Develop a scorecard for reporting these KPIs that meets HQ and local market requirements.
  - Make recommendations on research methodology given the nuances of the Hispanic segment and

potential opportunities for integrating brand tracking driving efficiencies for the brand tracker.

- <u>Work Stream #2</u>: Equity Tracker—Brand health measures to track for the Hispanic market
  - To develop a brand equity tracking system for Hispanic segment by agreeing on and defining key performance indicators for client at the HQ and local market level.
  - Develop a scorecard for reporting these KPIs that meets HQ and local market requirements.
  - Make recommendations on research methodology given the nuances of the Hispanic segment and potential opportunities for integrating brand tracking driving efficiencies for the brand tracker.

- <u>Work Stream #3</u>: Longer-Term Tracking Needs—Distribution, pricing, velocity, media spend by competitor by market, etc.
  - Identify other potential tracking needs for Hispanic segment (media, pricing, distribution by channel type, etc.).
  - Prioritize tracking needs based on cost / benefit analysis.
  - Make recommendations on methodology and suppliers for priority tracking needs.

Project Structure (Governance)

- *Project Lead*: _____ will be accountable for managing all resources to deliver results and coordinate across different work streams. He or she will be responsible for communicating project progress and bringing up conflicts and issues as they arise.
- *Project Manager*: _____ will work as the key day-to-day contact for Project Lead. _____ will work with Project Lead to on a weekly basis ensure

that priorities are clear for each work stream, and ensure the work plan aligns to those priorities, and review progress versus defined deliverables.

- *Steering Committee*: Steering Committee will consist of _____, _____, _____, and regional vice presidents from key geographies. Responsibilities will be to build commitment and mind share within the organization as senior advocates of the project, ensure alignment between functional and regional areas, and regularly check and approve direction of projects and resolve issues.
- *Core Team*: Responsible for executing / content development for each of the work streams. Within each work stream there will be a lead from Corporate Insights and the Hispanic team. These individuals will be responsible for managing their respective team members and ensuring that the deliverables are of quality and delivered on time.
- *Extended Team*: Will act as the final sounding board before any materials or recommendations get presented and will ensure that the needs of the Hispanic team and the regions / distributors are being taken into account.

ACKNOWLEDGMENTS

Transformational Hispanic Marketing would not have been possible without a number of people. I offer my deepest appreciation to all of them. I'd like to thank my daughter, Kaley, for being the first person to read an early manuscript and for giving me the confidence that "this has legs!" I'd like to thank my wife, Judy, for her editing help and insights. I'd also like to thank my son, Cole, for playing an integral role in the editing process and for helping me sort through all of the nuances in getting the book published. I would also like to thank Brian Baker and Rocko Spigolon, who provided invaluable support and coaching during the copy editing and cover design processes, respectively. I would also like to thank and acknowledge some of the people who have shaped my career. To Cindy Alston, who when I was just out of business school, entrusted me with my first and formative multicultural marketing role at Gatorade. To Bill Levisay and Jim Taschetta, two of the smartest marketers I had the benefit of learning from while at The Coca-Cola Company. To Sergio Zyman and Randy Ransom, the two very intense and brilliant Mexican bosses who taught me more than anyone about marketing to Hispanics. To all of the

Brandiosity clients over the years, thank you for your trust and your business.